Mother Knows Best

pil

Publications International, Ltd.

Contents

Mother Knows Best isn't just laden with how-to information and tips to solve all the world's problems, it also contains cherished memories from the history of motherhood, jokes and quotes from all of mothers' biggest supporters (their families), and stories of intuition, love, and gratitude. We move from the emotional to the practical chapter by chapter, giving you a glimpse into the omniscient and omnipresent forces of "Mom."

As you've heard all your life, your mother really does know best, and this book proves it. Have access to all of the information you disregarded as a child in this one book. *Mother Knows Best* will answer all your questions about how best to approach the world when things get messy, chaotic, or confusing.

CHAPTER 1

A Mother's Test in Greatness

Mothers are tested every day by their challenging children. It's not to say that they do not love their children, but, nonetheless, their children can be a handful of frustration that would peeve the calmest and most indifferent of people. They are faced with temper tantrums, absentmindedness, an onslaught of supposed needs and wants, criticism, high expectations, messy houses, and unkempt yards, but somehow they are able to rise above it all in a composed manner to get the job done. Mothers do it all without a fuss. They are truly the greatest people in our lives that set the example for us all. Let's celebrate the mothers every where who pass the test of greatness everyday.

For the Love of Mom

Who doesn't love Mother's Day? As it turns out, the woman credited with organizing the first "official" Mother's Day wasn't a fan.

The ancient Greeks worshiped the concept of motherhood. Rituals that honored Rhea, the mother of the gods, took place in spring and were said to be wild ecstatic parties full of drumming, dancing, and drinking. The Roman version of this festival—Matronalia, which was dedicated to Juno Lucina, the goddess of childbirth—was not as wild, but a Roman mother could at least expect some gifts. With the advent of Christianity, such festivals disappeared, but eventually the church also provided a way to honor mothers.

In the 16th century, the fourth Sunday of Lent was set aside as "Mothering Sunday," a time when people were expected to visit the church where they were baptized. This day ultimately became a family reunion of sorts. Back then, many children were sent away from their parents to work as apprentices or servants. Their visits home for Lent were known as "going a-mothering." The children would bring their mothers wildflowers or small presents. "Mothering Sunday" is still celebrated in Ireland and parts of the United Kingdom.

From Mothering Sunday to Mother's Day

Today, if you are anything like 96 percent of the American public, you participate in Mother's Day by spending money. Mother's Day is one of the biggest gift-giving holidays of the year. In fact, we spend more only during the Christmas season. Interestingly, the holiday got its start from a group of early feminist activists.

During the American Civil War, a woman by the name of Ann Reeves Jarvis formed "Mother's Day Work Clubs" to help improve living conditions (among other things) for soldiers on both sides of the conflict. Her efforts inspired the suffragist Julia Ward Howe (who was famous for writing "The Battle Hymn of the Republic") to call for a "Mother's Day for Peace." Howe was convinced that if women had been running things, the horrors of the Civil War could have been prevented. In 1870, she wrote a "Mother's Day Proclamation" that urged women to unite against all war. But neither woman's efforts amounted to any official recognition of Mother's Day.

The cause gained new life in 1905, after Ann Reeves Jarvis's death. Her daughter, Anna M. Jarvis, took up the "Mother's Day" mission—and it eventually took over her life.

This Wasn't What I Had in Mind...

It was Anna M. Jarvis's grief over her mother's death that most likely prompted her, on May 10, 1908, to stage what is considered to be the first "official" Mother's Day. She gave white carnations to each of the mothers at her church and encouraged her fellow parishioners to set the day aside as one of commemoration and gratitude. The idea spread, and in the years that followed, Jarvis lobbied business leaders and politicians for a national mother's holiday. Finally, in 1914, Woodrow Wilson issued a proclamation that set aside the second Sunday in May to honor mothers. The country quickly embraced this idea in a distinctly American way—by shopping.

The commercialization of Mother's Day enraged its founder. Jarvis saw what she'd envisioned as a holy day become another excuse to sell merchandise. In fact, when she saw "Mother's Day" carnations being sold to raise money for veterans, she tried to stop the sale and was arrested for disturbing the peace. She even filed a lawsuit to stop Mother's Day altogether. She died, childless, at the age of 84, regretting Mother's Day's existence. She never knew it, but her final medical bills were partly paid for by florists.

Dad asked Mom to tell him her most secret fantasy, and she told him she would like to have two men.

"Really?" Dad asked, surprised. He was just getting ready to tell her his own fantasy when she added, "One to do all the housework, and the other to run all the errands."

A Gift From the Past

My grandmother was a professor of English literature. Some considered this an academic step up from her mother, a high school English teacher. My mother taught freshman composition at a junior college while working on her doctorate. My grandmother often expressed how proud she was of all the teachers in our family—all the way back to my great-grandmother. Everyone assumed I would follow in the family footsteps; the only unknown was my academic focus. History or science would have been a new field, but literature would have been the traditional choice. All were worthy as long as they led to the teaching certificate. My grandmother would hang a copy of my certificate in her study along with her certificate, her mother's, and my mother's. We called it her trophy wall. In college, I chose education as my focus, but the thought of facing a classroom did not inspire me. By the time I was a junior, I had developed a passion for journalism. But I did not want to teach it, I wanted to do it.

My mother was not surprised by this. She had recognized my talent in the school newspaper I edited and read my passion for reporting between the lines of my articles. She said she was proud of me, and we would break the news to my grandmother together.

Sitting in her book-lined study, beneath her trophy wall, my grandmother poured tea and probed me about my studies. She pointed to the empty frame and noted that in a year, her wall would document four generations of women teachers. She pushed her glasses further up the bridge of her nose and smiled proudly. Finally, I found the courage to tell her. She did not say anything, just focused her attention on an edition of my newspaper.

Abruptly, my grandmother left the room. When she returned, her skirt was dusty and a wispy cobweb hung from her hair. She handed me a leather-bound journal that smelled of mothballs. The leather was cracked and the pages were yellowed. "This is your great-great-grandmother's," she said. "She would have been an accomplished journalist, but she had eight children and a homestead to run." I looked at the empty frame, still uncertain of her feelings. She smiled and said, "That's for your first prize-winning article. Don't make me wait too long." She handed the journal to me. "I've been wondering for years which granddaughter I would give this to."

A Second Child

When our second child was on the way, my wife and I spoke to our pediatrician about how to break the news to the older child. "Some parents," the doctor told us, "tell the older child, 'We love you so much we decided to bring another child into this family.' But think about that. Joanne, what if your husband came home one day and said, 'Honey, I love you so much I decided to bring home another wife.'"

Joanne considered this for a moment and then asked, "Does she cook?"

When I think of my childhood, I don't think of vacations and holidays as much as

ordinary times—learning
to do chores around the
house and having you help
me with my homework. You
made even ordinary
days special.

Mom, you are like a tree that stands in the
forest. You selflessly support the lives of those
who live within and around you, but when
your limbs are weak and you need a rest,
you make sure no one is around to hear
you fall.

The only one of your children who does not
grow up and move away is your husband.

A couple drove down a country road for
several miles, not saying a word. An earlier
discussion had led to an argument, and
neither of them wanted to give in. As they

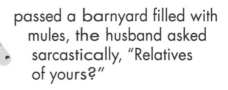

passed a barnyard filled with mules, the husband asked sarcastically, "Relatives of yours?"

"Yep," the wife retorted. "In-laws."

A What Dress?

My aunt, southern to the core, kept her promise to her deceased sister that she would be a mother to me, her niece. We seldom visited because she lived in Alabama, and I lived in Chicago. One day, I received a birthday gift that had me scratching my head. It was a dress patterned in pretty pastel flowers. It did not have zippers, buttons, or a belt. I reluctantly pulled it over my head and stared in the mirror. "Definitely not a nightgown and absolutely not my style," I thought. "At least not a style any woman I knew would wear for any occasion that I could imagine."

I called my aunt and thanked her for the—
I was hoping I had the right noun—dress.
I said it was exactly what I needed. But
I could not ask her what I needed it for.
She replied, "Every woman needs a fresh
doorbell dress, and it's not what you think to
buy when you're out shopping."

"I just love my doorbell dress!" I made
sure to emphasize my two new vocabulary
words. A Google search returned no
answers, so I hung the dress in my closet.
Occasionally, I found myself asking a friend
or colleague, "What's a doorbell dress?"
I gathered an impressive collection of
perplexed looks, but no answer. Several
years later at a national conference, I heard
a Southern drawl. I immediately thought
of my doorbell dress. Maybe she could
enlighten me. I walked toward her, and
blurted out my question.

"Why, sweetie, don't you know?" Her eyes
were wide with surprise.

I confessed to my ignorance of the doorbell dress, and of every woman north of the Mason-Dixon Line. She explained. "When the doorbell rings and you're in your grubbies—changing the baby or scrubbing the floor—before you open the door you just slip on the pretty, fresh dress hanging beside it."

My door-opening debuts immediately flushed before my eyes—tugging down my son's football jersey to cover my thighs; wrapping a throw rug around my nightgown; the talking head with my dripping, towel-wrapped body hiding behind the door; my baby-and-vomit look; my finger-painting phase; my covered-in-spaghetti-sauce conversation with a new neighbor.

After the conference, I rescued the mystery dress from a seldom-visited corner of my closet and hung it beside the door. I realized then that nothing could be smarter or do more for my pride than a doorbell dress!

Losing a Husband

My mom and dad came back from a lengthy camping trip, and when I stopped by to say hello, I was surprised to see that my mom was clearly not happy.

"Mom, is anything wrong?" I asked.

She sighed. "Well, Jane, some people say that losing a husband can be hard. In my case, it proved to be impossible."

I Didn't Wake You, Did I?

Mom and Dad had a big blowout that left each of them stewing in anger. For the rest of the day they gave each other the silent treatment. Before bed, however, Dad realized he needed to get up early the next day for an important meeting. Knowing that Mom was an early riser, he left her a note that said, "Stacy, please wake me at 6:00 a.m."

When he rolled over in the morning and saw that it was already 8:00, Dad was furious. He was about to go see why Mom hadn't woken him up when he noticed a note on his pillow. It said, "It's 6:00. Time to get up."

Herstory

Three weeks after her mom passed away, Shawna found the box. She and her brother, Joe, had been cleaning out their mom's house, sorting through what they would keep and what would be tossed out. It was a large box tucked in the back of her mom Ava's closet.

Shawna felt a fresh pang of grief and loss for the mom she had thought of as perfect. Ava had been one of those stay-at-home moms, straight out of the 1950's, completely devoted to her family, especially her two children. Shawna imagined how bored, and how boring, her mom's life must have been and vowed she would live a more exciting life if she ever married and had kids.

She opened the box and was surprised to find bundles of old newspaper articles, letters, and several bound diaries. She unwrapped one of the bundles and sorted through the articles. She was shocked to see her mom, a much younger Ava, in a photo next to a headline that read "Anti-war activist arrested at Kent State." Shawna read the article, her mouth hanging open as she read about how her own mother spent two days in jail for taking part in a protest.

"I don't believe this," Shawna whispered, as she began reading other articles, showing

Ava standing beside the likes of Tom Hayden, Jane Fonda, and Martin Luther King, Jr., at a civil rights rally! Shaking her head in disbelief, she read through one of the letters. It was a passionate love letter to her mother from a man named Leo. Shawna's dad was named Frank, and as she read other letters, Shawna realized that before her mom was married, there were many hot and heavy love affairs.

Shawna took out one of the diaries with a key attached and lovingly caressed the cover. She wanted to respect her mother's privacy, but she longed to know who this special woman, devoted to family in her later years, had been as a younger woman. As she read on she realized her mother was not boring, or bored, at all. She was a truly amazing woman, actively and passionately engaged in the world, who gave it all up to devote herself to her family.

CHAPTER 2

A Mother's Intuition

The bond between mother and child has symbolized the deepness and richness of family in narratives and folklore throughout time. The physical process of gestation is a daunting task that mothers have struggled with, creating life and relationships that bridge the harsh and cruel realities of nature. There is pain, suffering, overwhelming emotion, joy, revelation, and anxiety wrapped up into a single event that completely alters the lives of everyone involved.

For nine months, the whole family prepares for the new addition, painting and preparing the nursery, picking names, and choosing physicians and birthing locations. But all the while, the mother and child are bonding in ineffable ways, ways that are unnoticed by our senses. The mother feeds the child with all that she is. Everything that makes her stronger or weaker, satiated or wanting, is shared with the child in a symbiotic relationship that not even birth itself can fully break.

The mother's intuition is the continuation of this symbiotic relationship in the flesh between two individuals, leading to uncanny senses that have the mother running for help before she knows anything has gone wrong. Mothers always want to hear that you're doing well, but deep down, they know all the details you don't dare to talk about.

A mother's instinct tells her when to protect her young. Her intuition tells her when to let her young roam free. I thank you, Mother, for always knowing just when to hold me close and when to let me fly.

Forget What the Experts Say

Every time I see a new study by a parenting "expert" I have to laugh. I'm sure these people are properly credentialed and have done their best to discover something that will be of help to America's parents. But I believe that the real reason they're researching the effect of salt on infants' sleeping habits and which wall colors enhance your child's intelligence, is because even they are looking for answers. That's right—even these venerable professors, scientists, and doctors are clueless when it comes to what makes a good parent and a happy baby.

When I had my first child almost a decade ago, I was a dedicated, by-the-book parent. I read everything about pregnancy and childbirth that I could get my hands on. I swore off caffeine, choked down my prenatal vitamins, and aspired to be the perfect new mom. But as time passed, I realized that my son bore about as much resemblance to the babies described in the parenting manuals as my post-pregnancy body did to Angelina Jolie's. And the real questions I needed answers to—When will I feel like myself again? When will he sleep through the night? How can I get a shower in when he screams every time I set him down?—weren't in the books at all.

As my son grew, so did my confidence. Now that I'm the proud mom of three, I rarely pick up a parenting manual or read a how-to article. I've learned through trial and error how to make sure my toddler gets enough vitamin C to prevent scurvy with all-fruit popsicles, and it was pure chance that led me to the solution for morning clothing battles with my middle child (choose a school with uniforms!).

My attempts to keep my family healthy, happy, and safe may make the "experts" cringe. Because let's be honest, you won't find popcorn for dinner on the pages of any parenting book. The things that work for us aren't the same for any other family on the face of the planet. The only way to really learn what works for you is to try a little bit of this and a little bit of that. And then if you want to see what kind of job you're doing, turn to the real experts—your kids. Are they clean? Healthy? Reasonably happy? Then you get an A+ in my book.

❋ ❋ ❋

Mothers know how to create boundaries while still allowing us to choose our own path.

Following Your Gut

On July 31, 2014, beautiful twins, Aurora and Parker, were born to a loving couple, completing the couple's wish to have a family. The first year was filled with all of the ups and downs of parenting for the new parents. Although things were hard, all the checkup signs pointed to the healthy development for their children. The twelve-month checkup was positive and reassured the couple that all of their efforts were paying off. The twins seemed perfectly normal until Aurora began to develop a large, distended belly. At first, the couple would joke about her belly, thinking it was normal for babies to have a rotund belly, affectionately calling her "Buddha Belly." But deep down, the mother, Marie, began to think that Aurora's belly might not be so normal.

Thinking that she would wait three months for the next scheduled checkup, Marie began to notice the growing size and firmness of her daughter's belly. It was normal to have a little baby fat, but was it normal for it to be stiff and seemingly larger than what it should be? After a busy day at work, Marie came home to the two apples of her eye to get a glimpse of Aurora, and from that glimpse Marie knew something wasn't right. Aside from all the regularity of peeing, pooping, drinking, eating, and unrelenting cuteness, there was a dark underbelly to the situation that Marie could not put her finger on and did not trust. The call to the doctor's office confirmed that all the regular signs of health were present, but the worry in Marie's voice prompted the doctor to have her come in just in case.

Marie began to feel like she was being perceived as worrisome or neurotic as the doctor asked " So, Mom, what seems to be your worry." Was Marie overreacting? Was she building things into something they weren't? If all the checkups have come back positive, could there be something negative that was unseen? Marie expressed herself as calmly as she could, stating her concern and fright that she might be overreacting, but the doctor soon confirmed that something was, in fact, not right. "You might not get your answers tonight, but we are going to admit you for the next day and get you some answers," the doctor said.

After x-rays, ultrasounds, and a variety of other tests, it was confirmed that Aurora had a large growth within her abdomen and awfully high blood pressure. Within minutes of the test results, Aurora and Marie were taken to the Pediatric Intensive Care Unit for Aurora to be stabilized. The news was later broken that day that Aurora had cancer, and that the growth was known as a Wilm's tumor that was taking over her kidneys with the possibility of spreading to her lungs and heart. Marie was devastated and broke down in tears, calling her husband immediately.

The next eight months of their lives were filled with surgeries, daily visits to the hospital for IV sedation and radiation therapy, a twenty-five week chemotherapy regime, and heartache. Parker continued to develop, but Aurora was unable to sit or stand by herself, let alone walk, and suffered from brain damage from the chemotherapy. Things were very hard for Marie and her husband as they watched one child healthily develop and one child go through one medical hardship after another. But all was not in vain.

After nearly a year of various treatments, Aurora was said to be cancer free. They won the battle, but the war would continue for the rest of their lives. Aurora will continue to have x-rays every three months to make sure the tumor doesn't come back, and she may continue to experience side effects from exposure to chemotherapy at such a young age. After so much sorrow, the hope was not lost. Aurora survived her battle and Marie has learned to trust her instincts. Despite all of the social pressures and stigmas she felt from being perceived as an overprotective mom, it's because of those worries that her daughter is alive today. Although she thought she was making a big deal about baby fat, it was by trusting her gut that Marie was able to save her daughter.

Every successful person, every wise sage, and every masterful teacher who ever walked the earth started off as a child with a caring and attentive mother who taught them everything they know.

I had been feeling something ugly brewing for days—probably weeks—if I'm being honest. And by ugly, I don't mean the gray sunken circles under my eyes. Unfortunately, those are a given at this point. This particular kind of ugliness starts in the pit of your stomach and ends up as a worried furrow on your brow, exposing every forehead wrinkle you've ever had. Finally, as I hurriedly pulled the not-so-clean sheets over my bed and mentally went over all the things I unrealistically hoped to accomplish that day, the ugliness spewed out into a sentence that alarmed me—and finally brought some clarity. "I'm just too involved with my family."

I'm Just Too Involved...

I stopped tugging at the sheets and realized the absurdity of that particular combination of words. "Too involved." "With family." Always one to be thrilled with creating an oxymoron, this one just seemed sad to me. Is helping my children get ready for their first day of elementary school too involved? Is coaching my daughter's first cheerleading squad and doing a nightly load of grass-stained clothes from my son's football practice too involved? Is finally living up to the promise of a walk to the world's most patient black Labrador too involved? To top it all off, my husband doesn't even ask for any of my time at this point. He recognizes the bunched-up forehead and is steering clear.

That's when I heard it. The "ding, ding, ding" of the danger bells that always seem to peal at just the right moment, before I go over the edge and lose all sense of priority. In fact, at the very moment that I realized how much more important it is for me to nurture this beloved family of mine than to accomplish everything on my to-do list, I actually smiled. I smiled smack in the middle of a bedroom that needed to be dusted.

Suddenly I felt better than I had in weeks. One simple sentence that raced through my brain had freed me, for the time being, from the myriad of tasks that were plaguing my brain. Taking my kids for haircuts and new sneakers aren't tasks, they're privileges. Laundry and emptying the dishwasher are tasks. Sometimes we all just need a little reminder of the difference.

You never stopped doing things for me, even when I forgot to say thanks or show my appreciation. You never stopped trying to

help me, even when I ignored your sage advice. Thanks, Mom, for never giving up, even though the rewards have been few and far between.

A recent study from two psychologists at the University of Arizona has uncovered a particular finding with what some call "a mother's intuition." The study claims that when intuition is relied on more heavily than preference, women are able to accurately intuit the gender of their babies.

During the study, one-hundred pregnant women were asked to predict the gender of their baby. They were also asked if they preferred one gender over another and if their predictions were based on any outside information like a sonogram test. The result turned out to be quite impressive for the intuitive abilities of mothers. The study reports that 70 percent of the women in the test had correctly identified the gender of their babies with the use of intuition alone.

This may be surprising, but what surprised the researchers most is the influence that preference played in the study. Expecting mothers who had a preference to have a girl more than a boy or a boy more than a girl were less likely to accurately predict their baby's gender. The mother's preference or want of a particular gender knocked the mother's intuitive abilities out of whack, and thus the mother became less successful in using it. This may be good news for all of those kids out there who are suffering from high expectations from their mothers, and may teach mothers to expect less of their children and to come to terms with it. The researchers also commented that these abilities have a larger grasp on expecting mothers than they think. Dreams during pregnancy are now under scrutiny to find what they say about the mother's ability to intuit what character and personality traits their children will acquire.

Never Give Up

I woke up in the hospital emergency room cursing in front of my mother. Even now I cringe with fear of being grounded for using bad language, and I'm 42 years old.

I had been in an accident and had a fractured skull and various other injuries. Under the circumstances, my mother ignored my cursing, and I could see her face was white with the shock of seeing her child in so much pain. Looking back, I sort of wonder if it wasn't my colorful language.

In the days that followed, I was in more pain than I have ever known. Even after giving birth four times, the pain of my injuries was incomparable. So many times I felt as though I couldn't take any more. Yet every time I wanted to give up, there would be my sweet mother. Every time I awoke, she was sitting quietly at my bedside. And when she could see my frustration, my agony, she would distract me by talking about my sisters, about our neighbors, and about my friends who were so supportive. She talked to me about when I became a mother, patiently reminding me of all I had to look forward to. She quietly forced me to not give up.

She showed me that there is always good to counter the bad. She made me laugh and made me smile. And little by little, I got stronger, both physically and emotionally. I felt like I was slowly seeing the storm come to an end and the sun peeking out behind the clouds.

All these years later, I have been through my share of trauma with my own children, and I have had plenty of bumps along the road of life. Whenever things feel overwhelming, I think of my sweet, patient mother. I remember the way she single-handedly taught me to look for the good within the bad. She taught me that there is always light and hope in the world, and no matter how bad things seem they will always get better. And to never, ever give up.

Thank you for molding me with the loving hands of a mother and the masterful vision of an artist. Because of you, my life is a joyful masterpiece and a testament to your many wondrous skills.

Thank you, Mother, for being my compass. When I feel lost and confused by the world around me, I look to you for the guidance and direction I need, and I am found again.

The Smells of Comfort

Regina drove down the long tree-lined dirt road that led to her mom's farmhouse. Growing up on a farm had been fun as a child, boring as a teenager, and insufferable as a young woman aching to see and experience the big world outside the boundaries of her rural Indiana town.

Life in the big city of Indianapolis was much more exciting, and Regina wasted no time in landing a great job at a hot interior design firm. She even met a great guy to go with the job. But every now and then, the comforts of her mom's warm house called her back, always for short and sweet visits.

Now it was ten years later. After a painful breakup and the rotten news that her company was bankrupt and she was out of a cushy job, Regina could think of nothing she wanted more than to find some solace and comfort in her childhood home with her loving, doting mom. As she turned into the gravel driveway to the house, she could smell the fresh scent of newly cut grass and the earthy sweetness of hay stacked against a weathered white picket fence.

Once she neared the sprawling white and yellow farmhouse, Regina felt her entire body relax as the odors of home came out to greet her. Freshly baked bread wafted from an open kitchen window, where she could see her mom bustling about. As she walked toward the door, she smelled the unmistakable scent of apple pie, and it sent her back to the joys of childhood in a delightful flash. She had a vision of her and her mom baking together, wiping flour from their foreheads and laughing at the mess they were making in the cozy kitchen. Now Regina's life felt like a mess, and all she wanted was to see her mom. She didn't have to knock. Her mom opened the door and grabbed Regina into a warm embrace. Regina closed her eyes and let her mom hold her, feeling like a little girl again in need of comfort, breathing in the smells of flour and sugar in her mother's hair. In that moment, she knew everything would be all right. She was home again, with the one person who could make all the bad go away with nothing more than a hug and a piece of pie à la mode.

Thanks, Mom!

Thank you for always being there to hold my hand when I am scared, cheer me up when I am sad, and keep me company when I am alone. You are the one constant in my life, my true North Star.

I don't regret much in my life, but if I had to do it all over again, I'd probably take less advice from my friends and more from you.

CHAPTER 3

A Mother's Favorite Memories

Mothers cherish all their memories. They fondly remember all of those pre-parent years of elite social engagements, nights out on the town for dinner and entertainment, and vacations of uninhibited freedom. But then they had children, and all of those memories don't compare to the memories they've created with their little ones. Those moments of firsts are always on the list, but then there are those smaller, less eventful moments that pack incredible amounts of profoundness in them. Mothers hold on to these tiny moments of clarity and love with all their strength, because these are what keep them going and caring and loving. A mother's favorite moments are the ones that almost went by unnoticed, but—in true mom fashion—they were noticed, and they were cherished forever close to her heart.

Maybe With the Right Middle Name?

I hadn't realized that my five-year-old son had overheard his father and me discussing the new baby until my dad stopped by for a visit.

"Are you excited about a baby brother or sister coming?" he asked my son.

"I guess so, Grandpa. But I think the names Mommy has picked out are kind of weird. She said if it's a girl she would like to name her Elizabeth, and that's okay, I suppose. But if it's another boy, Mommy said they are definitely going to call it Quits."

Mothering is a losing battle. You lose your figure, your sanity, your social life. You often lose your patience. And from the very first day you look into those tiny little eyes . . . you lose your heart.

How Could You?

My daughter came home from
school very upset, and
said, "Emma says
you're the tooth fairy!
Is that true?"

I was caught off guard
and said, "Well, yes."

My daughter cried, "Mo-om! How could
you go out every night like that and leave us
here alone?"

—Sairey Gamp

Making up Over Makeup

The day my mother nearly blew up the house
was the day I convinced half of my high
school that she needed to buy a clue. Why
did every single one of my friends have
permission to go to Megan's party, but

45

not me? I stomped home, filled with nothing but self-righteousness. Not speaking to her for three days had not worked. Maybe the petition in my backpack, signed by 40 people in the junior class, would provide her that clue.

She did not greet me at the door with a hug and the usual questions: How was your day? Do you need help with your homework? The day before she asked me to choose dessert. I didn't answer and refused to eat the apple pie. My father ate my slice.

As I arrived home, her car was in the driveway. Was she ill? My rage evaporated as I ran to her room. Her door was shut. I knocked, but she didn't respond. I slowly turned the knob and walked in. She was sitting at her vanity with her head in her hands. Had someone died?

I hugged her, and she slowly raised her face. Something was odd about her eyes. It took me a few seconds to realize what was wrong. Her eyelashes and eyebrows were gone!

"Mom?" I said softly. Had she lost her mind?

"Your father is going to have a fit!" she exclaimed.

"He'll get you the help you need," I said, surprised by the adult tone in my voice.

"Erin, I don't keep much from your father, but this is one thing he can't find out about!" Her voice was strained as she explained how the furnace had gone out.

Instead of illuminating that dim corner of the basement with a flashlight to relight the furnace, she struck a match. "The explosion blew me across the basement and, well, you can see what happened . . . "

"At least you have your hair!" I said. Then I thought for a minute. "Remember the false eyelashes you wouldn't let me wear?"

She nodded. "I didn't throw them away." Relief washed over her face as I continued. "And between us, we have enough eyebrow pencils to take care of those . . . "

She hugged me hard. We applied our combined beauty skills and supplies as best we could. She still looked a bit different, but we doubted my father would ever notice the difference.

During dinner, he looked quizzically at Mom. "Your eyelashes look different," he said. "Have you been using Erin's makeup?"

"I forgot the gravy!" she cried without skipping a beat, tipping over her chair in her flight to the kitchen.

I burst in right behind her, our shoulders heaving with suppressed laughter while my father called from the other room. "Girls? Girls! The gravy is on the table!"

Sore Loser

"I am such a loser!" my son Evan exclaimed.

"No you're not!" I said firmly. "Why would you think such a thing?"

"I lost my ball, I lost my action figure, and I lost my favorite truck . . . I lose everything!"

Mother's Day With Marigolds

Easter in India, far from my children and grandchildren, was poignant. My new friends kept me busy from Good Friday through Easter Sunday with a Hindu wedding, parties, and sunrise service at the only church in the predominantly Hindu village. I had volunteered to work with a charity staffed by Indians for six months, and I was willing to give up a family Easter for the greater good of helping the poor improve their lives.

Their children called me "auntie." I had an Easter egg hunt for them, which required boiling eggs over my one-burner gas stove and dying them with local products. Their finds were more than colored eggs, they were the only lunch these children could expect to have. In the slum, two meals a day are unusual; most get by with only one.

As Mother's Day approached, I shared the tradition with the Indian women I worked with. I did not tell them that my heart was growing sick because my Mother's Day celebration would consist of only e-mails. I began counting the days until I could go home.

Mother's Day began with Sunday service, but my co-workers gave the rickshaw driver strange directions. Instead of going to my hostel room, we headed to the slum. It was not a work day, and why were the women giggling so much that they were covering their mouths with their saris?

They translated the huge banner at the slum's entrance, "Happy Mother's Day, Auntie!" More than a hundred people welcomed me to their community of thatched huts. Each child held one marigold, and I gathered them with hugs and smiles. A mother braided them along with other fragrant flowers, creating a beautiful lei.

They offered me a chair they had decorated like a throne and served me a meal of white rice and meat on a banana leaf. The children sang a song they had written in Hindi. A colleague leaned in and whispered

that in their language, the words rhymed.
The song greeted their auntie from the U.S.,
who today became a mother they love.

Back in my room, my sweet-smelling lei around
my neck, I read e-mails from my family back
home. It took me five paragraphs to describe
all the love I had received from people
whose language I didn't even know. After I
hit the send button, my weeks remaining in
India felt just about right.

Adam's Underwear

My son, Danny, was bored one day and
started looking through the books on my
bookshelf. He found a leaf pressed between
two pages and immediately ran off to find
me. "Mom, Mom! Can we go to church?"
When I asked why, he replied: "That guy
Adam? In the painting? I just found his
underwear!"

Hitting the Bottle

I was struggling to get the last bit of ketchup out of the bottle one day when the phone rang, so I asked my four-year-old daughter to answer it, and ask whomever it was if I might call them back later. This was her end of the conversation: "Mommy can't talk to you right now, Father Clark. She's busy hitting the bottle."

The Storybook Quilt

After my baby shower, I plopped down in my new rocker in the nursery that smelled of new paint. Around me, gifts frothed out of bags and boxes. My friends had given me nearly every item on my gift registry. The crib linens matched the pink curtains. The lamp and bookshelf went well with the princess theme. And so did the tiny pink shoes and storybooks about little girls in tutus and princesses in glittery gowns.

The only odd gift was from the person who should have given me the best gift of all, my mother. I pulled the hodgepodge of scraps from a pink gift bag. Mom had smiled proudly when I opened it. When I hesitated, she whispered, "Quilt." I forced a smile, muttered "Thanks," and continued to open the other gifts.

The quilt was large for a crib. Its patchwork of uncoordinated colored squares, circles, and triangles reminded me of the Little Match Girl, who was so poor that she wrapped herself in rags to sell matches on a snowy street. My daughter would be a princess, not a pauper! What was Mother thinking?

I was chilly and tucked the quilt around my huge belly. I began to slide my finger along a blue velvet patch. The feel of the fabric brought back a memory of me singing a solo at a recital when I was five years old. I remembered my stage fright, then Mom telling me to take a deep breath for courage, and exactly how it felt to sing my heart out. I noticed a triangle of green seersucker from my first day of school. I had torn it at recess, but Mom just hugged me harder and praised the "Good Job!" on my alphabet paper.

A dull brown patch was from my Brownie uniform. Mom had been our troop leader. Scattered on the quilt were circles of Girl Scout badges, too. Mom had been patient with kitchen disasters as I worked my way through my cooking badge. A bit of pink flannel told the story of my first sleepover. A square of green satin spoke of being my cousin's junior bridesmaid. I snuggled deeper into the quilt, imagining sharing stories from my childhood with my daughter.

I nodded off, wondering what other tales the quilt would tell.

That night, instead of reading one of my three new parenting books, I was eager to read more of my quilt. But first I called my mother to thank her for the best gift of all.

A Most Sincere Apology

What is it about boys who won't stop fighting? Mine are five and six and are at each other's throats constantly. One day, I overheard an argument that ended with the younger one calling the older one a dummy. I immediately put him in time out, where he cried his eyes out at the indignity. Afterward, I made him apologize to his brother. Reluctantly, he finally choked out, "I'm sorry you're such a dummy!"

Mother's Day Letter

"For Nick to read when he is grown," the envelope said. I have a tradition of writing letters to my kids at different times in their lives and saving them to read when they are older. This particular letter I had written to my son, now 21, was dated Mother's Day, 15 years ago. He had been in kindergarten, and reading it brought back memories of the day I realized what a truly selfless, kind child I had been blessed with.

Dear Nicholas,

Today was Mother's Day. As I watch your beautiful sleeping face, I wanted to write this letter to give you later so you will always know how much joy you bring me. You gave me the best present I've ever received today! It has a little story behind it that I will treasure forever. You have been diligently saving your allowance for weeks

to buy some material for Grandma to make
a tee-pee for you. You had $7.00 saved
last week, but you asked me to take you to
a nearby boutique where handmade crafts,
which I love, were sold. You were so cute
watching me as I looked at things, and if I
liked something, you would ask how much it
cost. We found an adorable little teddy bear
with an antique-lace collar, a ribbon tied
around its neck, and a ring attached. You
pretended you loved it and even tried on the
ring. You were very sneaky for a five year-
old! You bought the bear all by yourself and
said you were sorry because you spent
all your money and would just make me
something for Mother's Day. I would have
loved anything you made!

This morning you woke me up with a big
grin and a package wrapped in paper
towels and duct tape. You were so proud
and excited! Inside was the little bear that I
will always treasure. You sacrificed your tee-
pee for me.

I am so proud of your sweet, generous spirit
and the many ways you bring me joy every

single day. You are truly special, and I am honored to be your mother.
Love, Mom

I still have the bear and the little ring. And Nick did get his tee-pee. I smile at the memories and place my letter for Nick in an envelope to mail to him, hoping that reading it will remind him what a miracle he is and how blessed I feel to be his mother.

The Food Has Touched Down

The restaurant where our family went for lunch one Sunday was crowded because of a big NFL game on television. The busy server took our order, but quite a while went by before she even brought our drinks. Just as she was setting them down loud cheering broke out from across the room. "Hey," commented my 12-year-old, "I guess someone finally got their food."

My Name Is Peter Parker

My son was notorious for being the class clown. When the substitute teacher asked him his name he answered "Spider-Man"— to his classmates' delight. The substitute didn't find it quite as funny and demanded to know his real name. My son apologized: "Oh, I'm sorry. It's Peter Parker."

Hello
my name is

Whoops!

After a long day, I finally got a chance to sit down with a glass of wine. "Whew, I'm pooped!" I told my husband.

"Oh no, Mommy!" exclaimed my daughter. "In your pants?"

Well, When You Put It That Way

I received a call from my son's teacher. It seems that not only did he turn in the same report entitled, "My Dog," that his brother had written for the same teacher a year earlier, but he also gave a rather sarcastic reply when asked why he would attempt to do such a foolish thing.

"Oh, I am sorry, Mrs. Tyler. What exactly did he say to you?" I asked.

His teacher told me he had the nerve to say, "Well, of course it's the same report, it's the same dog, isn't it?"

Always on My Side

The news struck Jane like a direct blow to the stomach. Her New York-based company announced that half their sales force would

61

be relocating to Japan, and Jane was the sales director. Within two weeks she was expected to uproot her life and move to a foreign country where she barely knew the language or the culture. Her boss explained that learning Japanese would be easy once the team was settled in, but Jane was anxious and depressed, especially about leaving her aging mother Lil.

When she broke the news to Lil, Jane waited for the other shoe to drop. Her mom had supported her in every step of her career and never questioned her decisions, but Jane knew part of that reason was because as sales director, she didn't have to travel, but delegated that to her sales force while she held a cushy desk job. Now she would indeed be traveling, permanently, to another country. Lil just smiled proudly when Jane broke the news, surprising Jane, who was sure her mom would put her foot down about her daughter leaving her behind. In fact, Jane was certain Lil would become downright upset, begging her daughter not to leave her behind.

But Lil stayed quiet and supportive throughout the next two weeks, offering advice and courage as Jane packed and planned and worried and fretted. Often, Lil would calm her daughter just by saying, "It will all work out for the best," which seemed to be her personal motto.

The first week in Japan was exciting, but it was nerve-wracking getting to know her way around. Jane missed her mom and felt guilty about leaving her behind in the States, with only distant relatives to look after her. One night, Jane was in tears, having gotten lost in a town where no one spoke English. She finally found her way home when her text-message tone went off. Jane checked her text messages. There was one from Lil that simply said, "It will all work out for the best."

Jane smiled and picked up the phone, not caring what time it was in New York. Lil answered on the first ring, and Jane didn't even say hello before she burst out, "How would you like to come live in Japan with me?" Lil responded immediately, "I've always loved sushi!" Jane and Lil spent the next 15 minutes making long-distance plans to close the distance between them.

Someone to Pick On

My son came to me one day and asked if he would ever have a little sister. I was so happy, since his father and I had wondered when to share our big news with him. "Oh, dear, do you really want a little sister?"

"I sure do, Mommy," Sean replied. "I'm tired of teasing the cat—sometimes he scratches me."

CHAPTER 4

A Mother's Guidebook to Relationships

Mothers are professionals when it comes to maintaining relationships. From having to deal with your father and the in-laws to all those cliquey parents at the school, mothers have dealt with them all. They know when to give you a piece of their mind and they know when to be understanding. Mothers can be social butterflies or contemplative introverts, but either way, they know how to maintain courteous relationships that will last a lifetime.

When Mr. Right turned into Mr. Wrong and I was so afraid to tell you and Dad because you thought so much of him, your response was perfect: "Honey, we mostly loved him because you did."

How to Maintain Old Friendships

When you leave home and/or your childhood friends move away—heading to different colleges or pursuing careers elsewhere—you may wonder how best to preserve old friendships. Even though cities, states, or even countries separate you and your buddies, you can still keep in touch. Be proactive about keeping up with these friends, making a point to e-mail, call, text, or write letters whenever possible. Communicate regularly so you can stay up-to-date on each other's lives (and so that each time you call, it doesn't necessarily have to be a three-hour-long game of conversational catch-up). It's likely that you and your friends will undergo changes while you are apart; try to be as open and accepting of these changes as possible, both in them and in you. Practice mutual respect, forgiveness, and acceptance, and be sure to express gratitude for their friendships. As the children's song goes: "Make new friends, but keep the old. One is silver and the other gold."

Suddenly She Sees

A newlywed wife was complaining about her husband to her mother. "He's never home, and when he is, he never helps with the dishes, and he just doesn't seem to care about what I think. And he's so messy! He leaves a trail of destruction everywhere he goes. Why didn't I see this before we got married?"

Not wanting to get caught in the middle, the mother replied cautiously, "Well, dear, they say love is blind."

"Sure," replied the daughter. "And it's too bad marriage is such an eye-opener!"

Big Dipper Dreamin'

I won't do it this year, I thought to myself. I won't get myself worked in a tizzy all in the name of providing a memorable summer for my family. I'll keep the visions of beautiful picnic spreads under control and the reunions and amusement park visits and everything else that leaves me gasping for air as I try to find energy to shop for school supplies by Labor Day. This summer I vow to keep my planning under control, and my family will end up happier for it. Of that, I'm quite sure.

One moment stands out as the perfect example of having gone a tad too far with the tiptoe-through-the-tulips bit. It was late last August, school was about to start, and I couldn't help but to reflect upon our whirlwind of a summer to make sure that we had done everything I had set out to do. Boating weekends? Check. Amusement park? Check. Outings with cousins and grandmas? Check. Red, white, and blue buffets and ice cream cakes? Check. On paper it seemed that all of my efforts to create a perfect summer for my family were accomplished, but I had a gnawing, uneasy feeling. Did I take a deep breath and enjoy even a moment of it? Did I lie on the grass and watch the clouds float by? Did I check out the Big Dipper even one time? Nope.

This year I won't let that happen. I'm going to create a mantra to buzz in my ear should I start to forget. "I do not need to make star-shape finger sandwiches. I do not need to make star-shape finger sandwiches. I do not

need to make star-shape finger sandwiches."
Nor does anyone expect me to make
lemonade from scratch or remove every
telltale smudge of grass stain from my kids'
clothing. After all, a good slide into third
base needs proof, doesn't it?

As another chance at summer approaches
I'm forcing myself to reach for sidewalk
chalk instead of my annual check list. I'm
going to let mushy peanut butter and jelly
sandwiches replace pesto chicken. I'm going
to let bedtime and bathtime fall to the
wayside, and instead of watching my kids
catch fireflies, I'm going to join them. I'm
going to live in the present to create loving
memories for the future.

What to Do if You Make a Mistake

"To err is human," the old saying goes, and
it's true—nobody is perfect. We all make
mistakes, but handling them gracefully is a

key to mature adulthood. Here are four steps to follow the next time you blunder.

1. Admit your mistake. A mistake is compounded by a refusal to "own" it.
2. Apologize—and mean it. There's nothing worse than somebody who says "I'm sorry" when they obviously aren't.
3. Fix your mistake. If you make an error, figure out how to fix it and do so as soon as possible. Correcting your flub will help you learn—and will help make sure you don't make the same mistake the next time.
4. Learn from your mistake. Identify what went wrong. Even better, identify the underlying cause of the mistake. Was it a lack of concentration? A lack of know-how? A lack of confidence? Isolating and fixing the root of the problem will keep you from repeating that particular mistake as well as

other mistakes like it. Remember John Powell's famous words: "The only real mistake is the mistake from which we learn nothing."

Brooding and feeling sorry for yourself after a mistake isn't going to help anybody, least of all you. Once you've admitted the mistake and identified its source, move on to your next mistake. That's right . . . there will be more.

How to Spot a Lie

Most people tell lies every once in a while. In fact, 98 percent of teenage respondents in one study admitted to lying at least once. If it's a "white lie"—a lie designed to spare someone's feeling—it might not be a big deal. But big lies not only hurt feelings, they can ruin relationships—especially if lying becomes a habit. Psychologists suggest that you look for these clues:

1. Body language. Sometimes our bodies tell a different story than our words do. Liars will often cover their mouths, rub their noses, or otherwise fidget in inadvertent "avoidance" poses when they are lying.

2. Changing stories. Liars often get small details incorrect when repeating lies.

3. Eye contact. Psychologists say that most people make eye contact at least half the time. If a person avoids your eyes, he or she may be lying.

4. Cadence and tone. Is the person talking faster or slower than normal, or in a higher or lower pitch? This may be a sign of a falsehood.

According to a study at Portsmouth University in England, blinking might be the most universal sign of lying. Researchers found that liars blink less frequently than normal while telling a lie. Their blinking rate goes way up immediately afterwards.

Thanks, Mom!

All that I hope to someday give to my child,
you have given to me.
All that I hope to someday be in my child's
eyes, you are to me. Thank you.

Mom, my first lessons about love were
learned in your arms. Thank you for always
making me feel so loved.

Do Opposites Attract?

It depends. The best couples
balance each other's strengths
and weaknesses, according to
sociologist Susan K. Perry.
An extrovert and introvert
can make a good team. But
if you argue all the time,
that's not a good sign.

❉ ❉ ❉

Loving you has been my greatest investment. For all the love I've given you, you've matched it 100 percent and paid interest in the form of advice, security, encouragement, and laughter.

Advice From Mom

There are two types of men that make very good husbands: archaeologists and antique dealers. They will become even more interested in you as you begin to age.

Dealing With Embarrassment

Slipping on ice, falling down stairs, sending a lovey-dovey text message to "Mom" instead of your boyfriend "Tom," spilling ketchup down the front of your starched white shirt: There are myriad ways to mortify yourself. Try as you might to avoid awkward scenarios, remember that everyone is embarrassed at some point! So when you next embarrass yourself (it's not a question of if), here's how to deal. First, don't obsess over the incident or devote a ton of energy to replaying it in your head. Remember that eventually people will forget what happened and time will minimize the incident's impact. Apologize to the appropriate people, if necessary, but again, don't dwell on it. The adage, "This too shall pass," is true. If possible, whoop it up over your embarrassing occurrence: If you laugh, others who witnessed your "special moment" will likely

feel more at ease. Laughing will also help you to not take things too seriously and get on with your life.

Advice From Mom

"Whatever you may look like, marry a man your own age. As your beauty fades, so will his eyesight."

—Phyllis Diller

Bridging the Gap

When I had my first child, people warned me that it would be difficult, if not impossible, to remain close to my friends who didn't have kids. "Once you cross that line, there's no bridging the gap!" they warned me. "You'll be thinking diapers and preschool while they're heading off to Bermuda and seeing every movie on opening weekend!"

But as my son got older, and as one baby became three, I discovered that keeping up with these childless women was a piece of cake compared to trying to be close with others whose parenting styles are the antithesis of my own. There's the organic mom whose little treasure has never seen refined sugar, let alone allowed a gummy bear cross his pristine lips. There's the Pottery Barn mom whose house looks like a spread from an interior design magazine—and whose kids aren't allowed to wear shoes in the house and must submit to an inspection with a lint roller before they are granted access to the living room. There's also the hypochondriac mom who won't let her child come within 20 yards of anyone who has had a sniffle in the past six weeks.

I don't want to disparage other parenting styles—after all, I've got my own foibles and quirks—but I do want to admit that it is a struggle to make these relationships work, even if a compatibility test would give us a score higher than Courteney Cox and Jennifer Aniston. But if the friendship is worth it, I've found ways to adjust.

I smartened up and started planning events

without (gasp!) the kids, where moms could forget they were moms and concentrate on each other. I looked past the perfect family room and ban on red dye #5 and found the woman underneath, the person I could relate to and enjoy. And I learned to let my own parenting rules bend a little, when the occasion called for it.

Why do I go through all this effort? Because I figure we're only parents part of the time. There will come a day when that beautiful house is quiet, the cookie jar is empty, and the last temperature has been taken. And then we're not going to care who's tracking mud in the house or when our last tetanus shot was. We're going to need our friends.

How to Apologize

We toss around the words "I'm sorry" very casually in conversation ("I'm sorry to bother you"; "Sorry I missed your call"; "I'm sorry,

I'm running a little late";
etc.), but when you've
really messed up, how do
you convey that you're
truly sorry? Apologizing
meaningfully can be
difficult, but it's also
incredibly important and therapeutic. First
of all, you need to know for what you're
apologizing. Then, you must be sincere and
humble and take full responsibility for your
actions or words. Try to apologize at a time
and in a place that is best for the recipient.
(Muttering "I'm sorry" after an argument
then scurrying out the door is not the most
thoughtful course of action.) Avoid placing
blame or making excuses. Be prepared to
mend the situation or right the wrong, and
make sure you convey your desire to do so.
After you've apologized, be patient; don't
expect the recipient's mood to change
immediately. Ask to be allowed to rectify the
situation, if that's possible. Then be sure you
follow through and mean it.

If you have difficulty articulating your thoughts and feelings in a particular moment, try writing a letter of apology and reading it aloud to the person you wronged (or letting him or her read it). This is a good way to organize your thoughts and make sure you don't forget anything you want to say or how you want to say it.

How to Get Over Heartbreak

There's no magic way to mend a broken heart or bounce back from a breakup. Friends and loved ones will offer all kinds of advice and encouragement, but you may not be able to accept it at first. Give yourself some time to mourn the loss of the relationship, then stop wallowing and get back out into the world. Even if you're not quite up for social events, you need new experiences and new things to think about. Go somewhere you've always wanted to go; try a new hobby or plan a vacation. And lastly, go easy on yourself. It will take some time to retrain yourself to no longer replay the happier moments of your relationship on an endless mental loop. Time will bring relief— it just takes patience and perseverance.

Secrets on Love

The theory used to be you marry an older man because they are more mature. The new theory is that men don't mature. So you might as well marry a younger one.

❄ ❄ ❄

Momism: "It's just as easy to fall in love with a rich man as a poor man."

❄ ❄ ❄

Don't marry for money; you can borrow it cheaper.

How to Dump Your Significant Other

When you decide that it's time to end a relationship, do it with grace and tact—and don't do it in anger. This can be easier said than done, so here are some strategies to help you make as clean a break as possible.

1. Plan exactly what you are going to say, as well as when and how you are going to say it. Explain your reasons for ending the relationship in a straightforward but sensitive manner.
2. Do it in person. You owe it to your significant other to communicate face-to-face.
3. Give him or her time to process the information.
4. Hold back. The other person might become upset or angry, but you should stay calm and resist the urge to resort to name-calling or verbal abuse.
5. If you want to stay friends, accept that this probably won't (and shouldn't) happen right

away. You will eventually have to work out what a friendship might be like, if your ex agrees.

Staying Connected With Your Family After You Leave Home

Leaving for college or moving into your own place is a significant milestone on the road to adulthood. You'll be setting your own rules every day, probably for the first time. But getting established outside of the family home shouldn't mean cutting yourself off from the family. It's important for you—and for them—to stay in touch. You'll need to find a balance between enjoying your new freedom and maintaining contact with your family. Here are some tips.

1. Social networks. Being "friends" with your parents and siblings on social networks such as Facebook is a great way to stay in touch. Your family can keep up with your life

without constant phone communication. Of course, you'll need to be careful about what gets posted on your wall.

2. Make time to call. Even a 15-minute phone call will let family members know that you care about them and want to be in touch.

3. Consult your parents—within reason. Believe it or not, your parents actually know a thing or two about life's ordeals. Asking them for advice—whether it's about how to make spaghetti sauce or a major life decision—is a great way to stay connected while transitioning into full-fledged independence. If you're worried about asking, remember that you're still free to take it or leave it.

CHAPTER 5

A Mother's List of Things
You Need to Know Before You Go

Mothers spend your whole life trying to prepare you for the real world, trying to make you as prepared as possible that day you walk out of the door for good. You'll have dreams and aspirations, career paths and connections to make, places to be and people to see. But none of it will matter if you don't take your mother's advice. Mothers have all the real world experience a person can get. They've been through it all before you even knew the light of day. After all of these years, you should know how to do your laundry properly, make reasonable decisions, and maybe even start a fire without matches. Some skills come easier than others, but this is the bare minimum of practical knowledge you need to know before you walk out of that door for good.

1. Food, water, shelter. 2. Vacations, designer jeans, video games.

It's pretty obvious which of these are needs (#1) and which are wants (#2); they're noticeably different. But have you ever considered the difference between needs and wants in your own life? How many times have you heard yourself say things like, "I need a latte!"; "I have to go to tour Europe before I die!"; or "I need a new tennis racket!" In reality, you probably meant, "I really want a latte," "I really would like to go to Europe," and so on.

Examining the difference between what you need and what you want can help you save money by living within your means. Taking inventory will make you aware of what you truly can't live without (hint: there's not much) and what are merely exciting "extras." You may think you can't live without cable or the latest model of mobile phone, but try it for yourself and see. While you can't—and shouldn't— erase all wants from your list, you can simplify. Consider perhaps a TV sans cable, or a more affordable, albeit slightly less "slick," phone model. You may learn that there is some freedom in simplicity.

Exciting news! Sometimes your wants can actually be things you need. Do you want a computer? Maybe you also need one for college. Similarly, you may want a cell phone but also need one for your job. Try to identify ways in which wants and needs intersect; they are worth investing in.

Take Control of Your Own Happiness

To take control of your own happiness, shift your focus to the things that make you happy! It can be easy to fixate on things that make you unhappy—a difficult exam, a tedious job, a speeding ticket, or a breakup, for example. But when was the last time you took inventory of all that's positive in your life? Make a list of who  and what bring you joy. These could run the gamut from a great meal to a meaningful conversation, a sun-breaking-through-the-clouds moment to a college scholarship. Another way to take charge of your happiness is to allow yourself to be human—to be in the moment and feel what you feel. Denying or rejecting your emotions only leads to dissatisfaction and disappointment. If your schedule is too full, learn to say "no" to things. If your plans are too complicated, simplify. Take care of yourself—mentally, physically, and spiritually—and in so doing, you'll take care of your well-being.

Managing Stress

There are countless situations that bring about stress: spreading ourselves too thin, encountering conflict in a relationship, experiencing financial trouble, holding ourselves 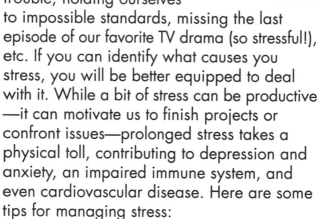 to impossible standards, missing the last episode of our favorite TV drama (so stressful!), etc. If you can identify what causes you stress, you will be better equipped to deal with it. While a bit of stress can be productive —it can motivate us to finish projects or confront issues—prolonged stress takes a physical toll, contributing to depression and anxiety, an impaired immune system, and even cardiovascular disease. Here are some tips for managing stress:

1. Take time off—whether it's an entire day or simply 15 relaxing minutes

2. Exercise or do a hobby that you enjoy to calm yourself down and feel rejuvenated
3. Write down what's stressing you out. Expressing your frustrations and worries on paper can be very therapeutic and help provide perspective
4. Talk to a friend or family member. They can provide perspective and encouragement. If necessary, seek advice from a health care professional.

Ten Things to Have in Your Car at All Times

For most of us, the car is a sort of traveling junk drawer, containing old papers, fast-food wrappers, clothes, sporting goods, and other sundry items. But if you have a breakdown in the middle of nowhere, is a frisbee going to do you any good? Here are ten items you should always have in your car.

1. Flashlight. Ever tried to change a tire in the dark? It's not easy.

2. Map. Even if you have a GPS unit, a good road map is essential.

3. Insurance card and registration. These are the things police officers ask for during traffic stops.

4. Blanket/warm clothes. It gets cold waiting for a tow truck in the middle of winter.

5. Cell-phone charger. At the bare minimum, you should have a cell phone charger that plugs into the cigarette lighter. Even better, stash a prepaid phone in the glove compartment for emergencies.

6. First-aid kit. Keep this beneath one of the front seats for easy access.

7. Jumper cables. Everybody leaves the headlights on all day at least once.

8. Road flares. Placed beside your car, these will alert other drivers that you are stranded and prevent them from hitting you.

9. Ice/snow scraper. It's hard to see out the windshield when it's completely covered in ice.

10. Nonperishable food and water. Even if you never get stranded for days, there will be plenty of times you'll be glad that you have water and snacks in the car.

While 911 is usually the best number to call for emergencies, many states have cell-phone codes with which you can report emergencies to the highway patrol. These vary from state to state, so it's important to learn which numbers work in your area.

There's a Fly in My Soup:

When It's Okay to Send Your Food Back at a Restaurant

You're at a fancy steakhouse for a special occasion, but when the medium-rare steak that you ordered arrives, it's so overcooked that you can barely cut into it. What should you do? Despite popular myths to the contrary, the majority of restaurants are very understanding—and apologetic—when a guest sends a dish back. Here are four situations when it's always okay to send back your meal.

1. The food is dangerous or offensive to you. If you have a food allergy or a religious objection to certain kinds of food, it's okay to ask the waiter to take it away, particularly if the menu doesn't make it clear that certain ingredients are in the dish.
2. The food is prepared incorrectly. If you ordered a steak done rare and it comes out looking like a hockey puck, you're perfectly within your rights to send the food back. The same goes for chicken, which should be cooked all the way through; undercooked chicken can lead to salmonella infection.
3. It's not what you ordered. Mistakes happen, even in the best of restaurants. Sometimes the server will bring the wrong dish, or perhaps he or she misunderstood what you were saying when you ordered. But there's no reason to force yourself to eat something

you don't want if you didn't order it.
4. There's literally a fly in your soup. Or
a bug in your salad. Or a hair in your
taco. Or any other foreign object where it
shouldn't be.

When ordering meat, don't assume that
the restaurant's idea of "medium-rare" is
the same as yours. When in doubt, ask the
waiter to clarify how the food is cooked.
Nothing incurs the wrath of a chef faster
than having perfectly prepared food sent
back to the kitchen. And nobody wants to
eat food cooked by a wrathful chef.

Memory Tricks

There's so much to remember these days:
names, birthdays, passwords, pin numbers,
addresses, project deadlines, bill payments,
and appointments, for starters. If you have
trouble remembering these and others, try
some of the following memory tricks.

Use your senses. Have you ever noticed the power of smell, for example, in triggering memories? You'll remember something much better if you connect it with multiple senses. Try to incorporate smell, touch, taste, sound, and sight—or as many of them as possible—to aid your recall.

Use your muscle memory. Yes, muscles "remember." That is why musicians play their instruments for hours and hours on end—so that they get to the point that their hands "recall" a certain motion or how to shift from chord to chord.

Use humor. If you can attach a funny word, name, or absurd mental cue to something you want to remember, you're more likely to recall it.

Practice! In the same way that you hone muscle memory, hone your mental memory by practicing. If you want to learn Spanish, practice conversing with Spanish-speaking peers. If you want to memorize a speech, practice it in front of a mirror or video camera.

Repeat. If you want to memorize a password or phone number, repeat it (or write it) over and over . . . and over and over and over . . .

How to Spot an Urban Legend

Okay, true story—this really happened to my dad's friend's brother-in-law . . . Wait, have you heard this one before? That's probably because it is an urban legend. Urban legends serve much the same purpose today as folklore did long ago; they are invented stories told to express fears or pass along moral lessons. Urban legends sound so believable that they can be difficult to spot. Here are a few telltale signs.

1. The story is about "a friend of my uncle" or "a cousin of a friend." Urban legends almost always take the form of an event that

has happened to a distant connection of the storyteller.

2. The teller insists it really happened. Think about it—when you tell somebody about something that happened to you, do you preface it with assurances that it really happened?

3. The story has a moral or an unexpected twist. Because urban legends are retold so often, they often take the forms of morality tales or pieces of folklore. If there's a "lesson" to the story, it might be an urban legend.

4. You've heard very similar stories before. How many people's cousins' friends could have had the exact same bizarre experience with a McDonald's chicken sandwich? The odds are not high.

5. It's an e-mail chain letter claiming "not to be a hoax." Oddly, just about every e-mail chain letter claiming not to be hoax actually is one.

Legendary Semantics

Urban legends are technically different from hoaxes, lies, or fallacies. Saying, "Barack Obama isn't American," is a fallacy, not an urban legend. But the classic story about the gas-station attendant telling the woman about the killer in the backseat would, in fact, qualify as an urban legend.

Know the Difference Between Facts and Opinions

Being able to differentiate between factual statements and opinions is a critical life skill. Today more than ever before, opinion masquerades as fact in print and over the air. Even textbooks are not immune to this distortion. Here's an example: "The new school dress code is not supported by 54 percent of the student body and will lead to students rebelling against it." The statement "not supported by 54 percent of the student body" is a fact (if the students were polled), but the statement "will lead to many students rebelling against it" is an opinion—no one knows for sure whether this will occur. Pay attention to language and ask yourself whether statements can be proved. Although certain words, such as "stated," "demonstrated," and "according to," are often clues to the presence of factual statements, they can be attached to statements to make them seem true. Watch out for descriptions that could be fact but often are opinion. A statement such as "The man was angry," is only fact if the man himself said that was his emotional state—perceptions are opinions, too. Be aware that writers can misuse language and, thus, misrepresent information. Don't accept any statement without questioning, and always check facts.

How to Start a Fire Without Matches

Warmth is almost as important to the human body as air and water. Knowing how to start a fire without matches could make the difference between life and death. You need two things to start a fire: tinder and heat. Tinder (the stuff that catches fire) can be anything that's dry and easily combustible—brown pine needles, dried leaves, or old newspaper can work. Heat comes from the sun, and you can use a lens to amplify its intensity. The lens can be a magnifying glass, an eyeglass, broken bottle glass, or even ice carved into a lens shape.

Pile the tinder in a flat, wind-sheltered place. If you can dig a small hole, that's even better. Next, generate heat. Angle the lens so that it concentrates the sunlight into a point and direct it onto the pile of tinder. Eventually, you should see smoke coming from the tinder; blow gently on it to encourage the flame. Once it combusts, add kindling such as small twigs or branches to make the fire larger.

Of course, this only works on a sunny day. If it's cloudy or dark out and there's an automobile nearby, you can get a spark from its battery. Take two pieces of wire and attach each to one of the battery terminals. Collect some tinder and bring it over to the car. Touch the wires together, right over the tinder—there should be a spark, which will make the tinder smolder. Blow on it and continue as above.

Fiction About Friction

In the old movies, people always started fires by rubbing two sticks together. Unless you have absolutely no other option, avoid this friction-based fire-starting technique—survival experts say it's the most difficult way to get the job done.

How to Use a Compass

You don't need to be a Boy Scout or wilderness guide to know how to read a compass. You may rely on the Web or a GPS (Global Positioning System) unit for navigation purposes, but these tools won't always be available to you. To read a compass, first you must find north. No matter what kind of compass you use, one end of the needle—usually the red-colored end—points north, so rotate the compass until the red end lines up with "N." For accurate compass readings, make sure that you keep the magnetic red end lined up with North at all times. If you are reading a map, rotate it so that north on the map lines up with the "N" on the compass.

Lunar Locator

You can use the moon to find the general direction of true north. If the moon rises before sunset, its bright side is in the west; when the moon rises after midnight, its bright side is in the east. Once you've established these directions, you can easily figure out which way is north.

How to Care for a Piercing

Getting a piercing can be a fun way to express yourself, but it's not so fun if you get an infection. With proper care, however, you can avoid infection and help the piercing heal correctly. Always wash your hands with soap and water before touching your piercing—it's the easiest way to stay infection-free. Don't touch the piercing or jewelry except to clean it. Different sites require different cleansing methods, but general directions for a skin piercing call for using a cotton swab dipped in warm water to remove any crusted discharge. Several times a day, dip a cotton ball, cotton swab, or piece of gauze in liquid antibacterial cleanser (avoid creams or astringents) and gently clean around the piercing site. Rotate the jewelry so that the cleanser is worked into the opening. Keep clothing from rubbing the piercing, and don't press a phone receiver against an ear that recently has been pierced. If you have any signs of infection—such as pain, swelling, inflammation, or yellow pus—seek medical attention immediately.

Avoid Astringents

Do not apply hydrogen peroxide, rubbing alcohol, or tea-tree oil to a new piercing! Hydrogen peroxide kills white blood cells, which are critical to the healing process, and rubbing alcohol and tea-tree oil dry out the skin, which can prolong the healing time.

CHAPTER 6

A Mother's Green Thumb

Mothers have an uncanny ability to grow things—from kids to flowers. It is a mother's nature to nurture and give sustenance to those that depend on them. The mothers of prehistory were responsible for growing and cultivating food as the men of the community went into the wilderness for game. Although men have been attributed with creating and greatly contributing to society, it is women who made the greatest contribution of all. Women invented agriculture and it is with agriculture alone that we were able to begin to form our advanced civilizations. With a woman's patience, humanity was able to learn the slow traditions needed for growing and supplying food. If it were left to the men, we would have continued to hunt and gather up to this day, remaining impatient and hostile as the natural world continued to thwart us at every step. The nurturing secrets of agriculture and gardening have been passed down perennially from mother to daughter through the ages, allowing our society to thrive under the harsh conditions of the wild. Although we are long past our need to individually grow food to survive, gardening and planting is an incredibly fulfilling and creative pastime that has us outdoors digging in the dirt like kids.

Take Gardening in Stride

Every successful plan must be grounded in reality. Take time to analyze your growing conditions: sun, shade, soil type, climate, and moisture. No plant, no matter how expensive,  will look good if it is suffering. Growing conditions can be altered but only to a certain extent. The ideal plan is a balance between the plants you want and those the conditions can support.

To prevent wasted effort, think about your goals first. Do you want to improve the front entrance? Repair the lawn? Make an outdoor seating area? Grow herbs or perennials? Add some shade trees? This is not all going to happen in one day. Approach the tasks in the right order. Plants thrive in healthy soil, not compacted clay or plain sand, so soil may need significant improvement. Trees take precedence over other plants because they take the longest to reach full size. If you want to have your lot terraced, have the construction completed first so that your garden doesn't get squashed by equipment. If you can't afford the terrace yet, grow grass in its place, surround it with a flowerbed of annuals, and plant starter perennials to divide later. Quick projects such as doorway planter boxes give an immediate reward but still fit into the long-term plan.

Different gardens suit different needs, so be sure to consider the functions of your space before you begin. Do you want to create a safe play place for your children, perhaps with room for a swing-set or sandbox? Do you have household pets that also need a share of the yard space? If you travel frequently, you'll need easy-care features and plants and possibly automated watering. Perhaps you want to reserve an area for outdoor entertaining with plenty of tables and chairs and a barbeque grill. Don't forget to take the style of your property into consideration as you plan. A large, formal house calls for compatible landscaping, but a cute little cottage from the '30s can get away with whimsical accents.

Also consider the amount of maintenance you would like to perform. A water garden might seem like fun, but will the upkeep be a nuisance? Do you enjoy harvesting cherries, or will you be disturbed by dropping fruit and wasps? An organic vegetable garden can be a priority to one person and an annoyance to another—let's hope you're not married to each other!

Ask Mom

Q: Mom, what is organic gardening, and does it really work?
A: Organic gardening is popular today, and for good reason: It works wonderfully! Organic gardeners shun the use of synthetic

chemicals to keep their yards free from potential hazards. But the real success of organic gardens lies in the methods used to keep plants growing vigorously, without a heavy reliance on sprays. Organic gardening cuts right to the heart of the matter: soil. Soil is the life force of the garden. When enriched with organic matter, the soil becomes moist, fertile, and airy—ideal for healthy plants. It also nourishes a rich population of beneficial organisms such as earthworms and nutrient-releasing bacteria. And it harbors root-extending fungi that help make growing conditions optimal.

Organic gardeners also stress problem prevention in the garden. Putting plants in the right amount of sun, along with suitable soil, proper spacing, and ideal planting and watering, allows most plants to thrive with minimal upsets.

The Right Growing Conditions

Plants have evolved all over the world, adapting over the course of time to local conditions, whether temperate or tropical, wet or dry, loamy or rocky, sunny or shady. Plants that failed to find a niche became extinct and vanished. These days, we bring plants from diverse climates and communities into our gardens. Even when we try to design with native plants, we know that they, too, have diversity in their history. Their

seeds may well have been brought to the region hundreds of years ago by animals, water, wind, and native people. Each plant species has a range of conditions under which it will thrive, other conditions under which it will merely survive, and unique limitations that will cause its death in hostile conditions.

Heat and cold influence plant survival. Understanding temperature in your garden will help you find the varieties of plants that can thrive for you, especially those plants that normally live for more than a year. Conditions in your garden are influenced by your region's climate, including frost dates and your garden's unique exposure. Plants can be grown outside their natural climate if you provide warmth to tropical plants in winter (for example, growing a lemon tree in a greenhouse in Massachusetts) or cold to plants from temperate climates in winter (for instance, treating tulip bulbs with weeks of refrigeration before planting them in Georgia). Consider both heat tolerance and cold tolerance before you select your plants.

The United States Department of Agriculture Plant Hardiness Zone Map divides North America into 11 zones based on average minimum winter temperatures, with Zone 1 being the coldest and Zone 11 the warmest. Each zone is further divided into sections that represent five-degree differences within each ten-degree zone. This map should only be used as a general guideline, since the lines of separation between zones are not as clear-cut as they appear. Plants recommended for one zone might do well in the southern part of the adjoining colder zone, as well as in the neighboring warmer zone. Factors such as altitude, exposure to wind, proximity to a large body of water, and amount of available sunlight also contribute to a plant's winter hardiness. Because snow cover insulates plants, winters with little or no snow tend to be more damaging to marginally hardy varieties. Also note that the indicated temperatures are average minimums—some winters will be colder and others warmer.

Ask Mom

Q: Mom, there's a spot in my garden that always stays soggy, and I can't grow grass there. How can I fix it?

A: Turn a low, moist spot into a bog garden for plants that need extra moisture. You can even excavate down a little to create a natural pond. Plant the moist banks with variegated cattails, sagittaria, cardinal flower, hostas, ferns, bog primroses, marsh marigolds, and other moisture-loving plants.

Watering Your Garden

At least 90 percent of every plant is water. No plant can live without some moisture, and certain plants use it in amazing ways. Orchids and bromeliads that live on tropical trees absorb rainwater through their foliage. Succulent plants and cacti store reservoirs of water in their swollen stem tissues so they can go for a month or more without rain. Prairie flowers such as butterfly weed store water in their fleshy taproots. And daffodils store water in their bulbs.

Without water, plants wilt and die. But too much water can be as bad for plants as not enough. If land plants are submerged in water for too long—even if just their roots are submerged—they may rot or drown from lack of oxygen. Balancing plants' water needs is like having a healthful diet. Everything should be consumed in moderation. Provide your plants with enough water for good health, but don't flood them with it. Most plants prefer steady moisture in the soil, especially in spring, so they can grow without interruption.

It is rare for nature to provide exactly the right amount of water, not too much nor too little, for garden plants. You'll probably have to water your plants during dry spells to keep them looking their best. You can also observe your region's normal rainfall patterns and choose plants that are appropriate. For instance, bulbs like tulips and daffodils come from regions with wet winters but dry summers. North American wildflowers such as Virginia bluebell tend to bloom early, during moist weather at a time when tree leaves are just emerging, and then go dormant, sitting out summer in dry shade. For this reason they are referred to as ephemerals. Subtropic areas, such as parts of Florida, have frequent storms in the summer rainy season, bringing floods of rain. During interruptions of the usual pattern, fast-growing plants may need extra water.

To monitor rainfall patterns, set a rain gauge in an open area of the garden. You can purchase one at a garden center or use a topless coffee can. After each rainfall, check the depth of the rain inside. A commercial rain gauge is calibrated and easy to read. To read rain levels in a coffee can, insert a ruler and note how high the water has risen. Then keep this information in mind as you choose your plantings.

As a general rule, most plants and lawn grasses need an inch of water a week. The idea is to keep the soil lightly moist and to prevent it from drying out completely, which can be damaging to most plants. However, plants don't always follow the rules, so here are exceptions to this guideline:

🐾 Hot weather, dry sandy soil, or crowded intensive plantings or containers may require more than an inch of water a week.

🐾 When the weather is cool, the plants are widely spaced, or the soil is heavy and holds moisture well, less water may be required.

🐾 Young or new plantings require more moisture at the soil surface to help their budding roots get started. Water lightly and more frequently to accommodate their needs.

🐾 Mature plantings with large root systems can be watered heavily and less often than younger plants. The moisture soaks deep into the soil and encourages the roots to thrive.

Some plants need more water than others, so choose plants with similar needs and plant them together. This way, you are not planting water-hogging impatiens next to dryland plants and trying to keep them both happy at the same time. Keep the water lovers in the wetter exposures of your garden or near your garden hose. Drought-tolerant plants can be grouped in areas farther from your sources of water. Moisture-loving plants include Louisiana and Japanese irises, foamflowers, marsh marigolds, Solomon's seal, sweet flag, horsetails, swamp hibiscus, cardinal flower, hostas, mosses, and ferns.

Avoid watering disease-susceptible plants at night. If water sits on plant foliage for hours, it can encourage fungal diseases to attack leaves, buds, flowers, and fruit. Plants susceptible to leaf spots, fruit rots, and flower blights are best watered in the morning, when the warming sun will quickly dry the leaves and discourage fungus development.

If you don't have the loose, dark earth of those fabulous gardens you've seen on television and in magazines, don't despair. It can be created by improving your existing soil for fertility and good drainage. Soils can be amended with sand to make them looser and drier or with clay to make them moister and firmer. They can be given plentiful doses of organic material —old leaves, ground-up twigs, livestock manure, and old lawn clippings, plus appropriate fertilizer. Organic matter improves and nourishes any kind of soil, which, in turn, encourages better plant growth. Some soils are naturally pretty good, but others may need significant improvement if they are to support a beautiful garden.

Your soil texture checkup has shown the percentage of sand, silt, and clay in your soil, a good starting point for improving it. But you should also have your soil tested before you start adding fertilizers and amendments to it. This is in keeping with the old adage, "If it ain't broke, don't fix it." Sometimes unnecessary tampering with nutrients or soil acidity can actually create more problems than benefits.

Soil tests tell you the nutrient levels in your soil, a plant version of the nutrient guides on packaged foods. They also note pH and organic content, two factors important to overall smooth sailing from the ground up. To have your soil tested, call your local Cooperative Extension Service, often listed under federal or county government in the phone book. Ask them how to get a soil-testing kit, which contains a soil-collecting bag and instructions. Follow the directions precisely for an accurate report.

The results may come as a chart full of numbers, which can be a little intimidating at first. But if you look carefully for the following, you can begin to interpret these numbers:

🐾 If the percentage of organic matter is under 5 percent, the garden needs extra compost.

🐾 Nutrients will be listed separately, possibly in parts per million. Sometimes they are also rated as available in high, medium, or low levels. If an element or two comes in on the low side, you'll want to add a fertilizer that replaces what's lacking.

🐾 Soil pH refers to the acidity of the soil. Ratings below 7 are acidic soils. From 6 to 7 are slightly acidic, the most fertile pH range. Above 7 is alkaline or basic soil, which can become infertile above pH 8. Excessively acidic and alkaline soils can be treated to make them more moderate and productive.

🐾 Add only the nutrients your soil test says are necessary. More is not always better when it comes to plant nutrients. Don't feel compelled to add a little bit more of a fertilizer that promises great results. Too much of any one nutrient can actually produce toxic results, akin to diseases or worse. Buy only what's required and save the rest of your money for a better use, like more plants. However, you can use lots of compost, the more the better, in most cases.

If your soil test indicates that your soil is very acidic, consider growing acid-loving plants, or try ground limestone to raise the pH. Limestone is nature's soil sweetener, capable of neutralizing overly acidic soils. It's best to add limestone in the fall to allow time for it to begin to dissolve and do its job. The amount of limestone you use will vary depending on the specific soil conditions. Don't dump limestone on soil randomly, because you run the risk of overdosing the soil with lime. Follow guidelines on the limestone package or on your soil test. Maintaining the new and improved pH is an ongoing project. Recheck the soil's pH every year and continue to add limestone as needed.

If, on the other hand, your soil test shows that your soil is on the alkaline side, add cottonseed meal, sulfur, pine bark, compost, or pine needles. Garden sulfur is a reliable cure when added as recommended in a soil test. It acidifies the soil slowly as microbes convert the sulfur to sulfuric acid and other compounds. Soil amendments such as compost, decaying pine bark, and ground-up pine needles gradually acidify the soil while improving its texture.

The Plants

Landscape plants available in the United States and Canada are generally of high quality. Whether you make your purchases through a local greenhouse or nursery, a mail-order specialist, a chain store, or a roadside stand, you'll usually find vigorous,

 insect- and disease-free plants. What's more, with rare exceptions, these offerings can be relied upon to be correctly labeled. Because of this consistently good quality, it's possible to buy plants wherever you find the best price on the variety you want. Bedding plants and perennials are generally sold in packs and small containers. Unless you need to evaluate the color of the flowers, the presence of blooms is unimportant. In fact, annuals that are not flowering in the pack tend to establish root systems quicker than those that are in bloom, resulting in side branching and abundant flowering. To ensure an easy transition from the greenhouse to the garden, purchase plants at nurseries or garden centers at the proper planting time. Good plants are stocky, not leggy, and have healthy green

leaves. They are not root-bound (having matted roots and too big for their pots), so the roots are ready to stretch out and grow in your garden. One way to check is to see if roots are already growing out the bottoms of the market packs.

Although plants are usually grown well, they are not always treated well at supermarkets and other places that do not specialize in live plants. Try to get them shortly after delivery from the greenhouse source, or purchase only from stores that keep tabs on the needs of the plants.

Young annuals are tender. If these plants will sit for a few days before you have time to plant them, be sure to attend to their needs for light, warmth, and water. Keep them outside in bright light but protect them from the strong afternoon sun and from high wind. Check the soil moisture daily; bedding plants dry out quickly and require regular watering. Each time bedding plants wilt, some of their strength is lost.

Trees, shrubs, and vines that have been grown in containers may be purchased and planted any time the ground isn't frozen. Moving a plant from a container to the garden does not shock the plant as does digging it up from a nursery row. Look for plants with vigorous growth that are well rooted but not crowded in the container and have no visible signs of pests or damage.

Landscape plants that have been dug from the nursery and have had their root ball wrapped in fabric are referred to as "balled and burlapped" (B&B). Purchase B&B plants only during spring and fall—their root systems are most actively growing at those times and are able to overcome the shock of disturbance. Pick plants that appear to have been freshly dug. A loose ball of roots indicates damage—choose another specimen. Choose trees carefully. By the time they are big enough to purchase, their trunk shape and branching habit have been determined. If there is a problem, it may not be correctable.

Ask Mom

Q: Hey, Mom, I'm looking for a particular cultivar that I can only find through mail order. Is it safe to buy plants from another temperature zone?

A: If you know the type of plant will grow in your climate, you should have no problem, honey. If the nursery's zone is warmer than yours, specify a safe ship date for your area. The newly installed plant will have all summer to acclimate to your seasons and should survive the upcoming winter.

Q: Mom, you know those large patio containers of trees and shrubs I have. How do I overwinter those containers?

A: Well, you should remove the annuals from the containers at the end of the season. Move the containers to a location protected from the warming sun and winter wind. Insulate the soil with mulch-compost, bark, or leaves—and make sure the containers receive adequate water during dry spells. In fall when you move the pots, try planting some spring flowering bulbs in them in place of the annuals, to enjoy some early season color next year.

Plants From Seed

There are many good reasons to grow plants from seed and as many ways to do so. Each type of plant has its unique seed. It is designed to grow but will only be coaxed to sprout in an environment that seems to offer life support to the plant. It's a challenge to meet the special needs of certain types of seeds but easier with others whose requirements are more straightforward. Be sure to read seed packet instructions. You can start seeds indoors or out, during different times of year. There is more than one right way to handle most types of seeds.

Indoors you have more control over growing conditions and a lot of flexibility about what time of year to plant the seeds. Use specially prepared seed-starting medium, which is available from mail-order seed companies and from garden centers. Start seeds indoors under lights, rather than in a window, for even, compact growth. Seedlings must have bright light from the moment they peer up out of the soil or they will be weak and leggy. In climates with cloudy weather or homes without south-facing windows, sun may not be reliable enough. A light garden is an ideal solution.

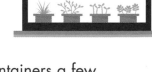

Set seedlings in their containers a few inches below a fluorescent shop light. You can place seedlings on a table or counter and suspend the shop light from the ceiling over them, or set up three or four tiered light stands. You can adapt ordinary shelves by attaching lights to the bottoms of the shelves and setting growing trays below each light. Put the lights on a timer set to turn on 14 hours a day and then off again (one less job for you). You can't beat the results! Make a mini-greenhouse under lights with a clear plastic garment bag. This traps humidity near seedlings, helping to protect them from wilting. To cover nursery flats full of seedlings, bend two wire coat hangers into arches and prop them in the corners of the flat, one at each end. Work the plastic over the top of the hangers, and tuck the loose ends in below the flat. It's even easier to make a greenhouse cover for individual pots. Slide two sticks into opposite sides of the pot. Then top with the plastic and fold it under the pot.

If starting seeds in a window, take extra care to maximize light. Use a south-facing window that will receive sun all day. It should not be blocked by a protruding roof overhang or an evergreen tree or shrub. (If you don't have a south-facing window, you should consider using plant lights.) Hang foil reflectors behind the flat to keep seedlings from leaning toward the sun. If the seedlings are sitting on a windowsill, make a tent of foil behind them, with the shiny side facing the seedlings. This will reflect sunlight and illuminate the dark side of the seedlings. They will grow much sturdier and straighter as a result.

Don't transplant seedlings into a larger pot until they have one or two sets of true leaves. This allows seedlings to develop enough roots to be self-supporting, even if a few roots are lost in the process. It's also a time when seedling roots are fairly straight and compact, making them easy to separate from nearby plants. This is not as simple as counting the number of leaves on the stem, however, because the seedling usually has an extra set of leaves called cotyledons. They emerge first and store food that nourishes the sprouting seedlings. Looking closely, you can see that cotyledons are shaped differently from true leaves. Squash seedlings, for instance, have oval cotyledons, but the true leaves are broad and lobed. When transplanting, handle the seedlings by the cotyledons to prevent squashing the delicate stem.

There are times to plant seeds directly in the garden. When this is successful, it is economical and very effective, for the plants grow without the disruption of being transplanted. Prepare the soil for planting and be sure the plot is fertile and smooth. Make rows or wide swaths for the seeds, following the timing and spacing directions on the packets. Straight lines help you discriminate between your plants and the weeds. The classic way to make straight lines is with posts and strings as a guide. Hoe along the string line for the shallow row. Plant seeds at the depth indicated on the packet and cover lightly with soil. Tamp down the soil over the seeds to make sure they are contacting the soil, and water them in. Be sure to mark the rows.

Many of the guidelines for indoor planting also apply to outdoor planting, but a main difference is pest control. Tiny plants are vulnerable to everything from aphids to chipmunks, so it's a good idea to plant more than you need and thin the plants later. Once they get past babyhood and are several inches high, thin them; they need space for the fast growth they are about to make.

CHAPTER 7

A Mother's Secret for Sickness Remedies

Mothers always know how to make their families feel better when they are feeling ill, from their perfectly toasted toast to the hot tea that is just sweet enough. Use this guide to lead you through your foggy head into a bright and beautiful day of cleared congestion and relieved fevers. You might think that moms are professionally trained doctors with degrees and practices of their own, but they are just caring and ingenious people. Here are some tips you can take with you when your mother isn't around to take care of you.

Most people know the symptoms of the common cold all too well. A cold is an upper respiratory infection caused by any one of hundreds of different viruses. The symptoms you experience as a cold are actually the body's natural immune response. In fact, by the time you feel like you're coming down with a cold, you've likely already been infected for a day and a half. Although Americans spend billions of dollars annually on doctor visits and cold remedies, there is no cure. Still, there are things you can do to feel better.

Rest. First and foremost, you should take it easy because your body is spending a lot of energy fighting off the cold virus. Staying away from work is probably a good idea too, from a prevention standpoint; coworkers will appreciate your not spreading the cold virus around the workplace.

warmth

Drink up. Nonalcoholic fluids may help thin the mucus, thus keeping it flowing freely and making it easier for the body to expel. When mucus is ousted, so are the viral

hot milk
with honey

particles making you sick that are trapped within it. Water and other liquids also combat dehydration. Drink at least eight ounces of fluid every two hours.

Cook up some chicken soup. One of the most beneficial hot fluids you can consume when you have a cold is chicken soup. Moses Maimonides, a physician and rabbi, first prescribed chicken soup for the common cold in twelfth-century Egypt and it has been a favorite folk remedy ever since. In 1978, Marvin Sackner, M.D., of Mount Sinai Hospital in Miami Beach, Florida, included chicken soup in a test of the effects of sipping hot and cold water on the clearance of mucus. To the doctor's surprise, chicken soup placed first, hot water second, and cold water a distant third. Physicians aren't sure exactly why chicken soup helps clear nasal passages, but many agree "it's just what the doctor ordered."

Use a saltwater wash. Molecules your body makes to fight infection called cytokines, or lymphokines, cause the inflammation and swelling in your nose when you have a cold. Research has shown that washing away these molecules can reduce swelling. Fill a clean nasal-spray bottle with diluted salt water (one level teaspoon salt to one quart water), and spray into each nostril three or four times. Repeat five to six times per day.

Gargle with warm salt water. Gargling with warm salt water (1/4 teaspoon salt in four ounces warm water) every one to two hours can soothe a sore, scratchy throat. Salt water is an astringent (meaning it causes tissue to contract), which can soothe inflammation in the throat and may help loosen mucus.

Vaporize it. The steam from a vaporizer can loosen mucus, especially if the mucus has become thick and gunky. A humidifier will add moisture to your immediate environment, which may make you feel more comfortable and will keep your nasal tissues moist. That's helpful because dry nasal membranes provide poor protection against viral invasion. If you don't have a vaporizer, you can drape a towel over your head and bend over a pot of boiled water—just be careful not to burn yourself.

Keeping It Cool During a Fever

Fever is not a disease in itself but simply a symptom of some other condition, usually an infection caused by a bacterium or virus. When such an enemy invades, white blood cells attack, releasing a substance called pyrogen. When pyrogen reaches the brain, it signals the hypothalamus, a tiny structure at the base of the brain that regulates the body's temperature, to set itself at a higher point. If that new set point is higher than 100 degrees Fahrenheit, you have a fever. When a fever develops, what should you do? Try the advice that follows.

Don't force yourself under cover. Shivers are your body's way of creating heat to boost your temperature, so if your teeth are chattering or you feel chilled, by all means, cover up to make yourself more comfortable. However, once your fever is established and you start feeling hot, bundling yourself under a pile of blankets will only hold in the heat and likely make you feel worse. You can't "sweat out a fever," or get a fever to break by forcing your body temperature up even higher. So if you feel as though you're burning up, toss off those covers or use a single, light sheet.

Undress. With your body exposed as much as possible, your sweat glands will be better able to release moisture, which will make you feel more comfortable. Strip down to your skivvies—that means a diaper for an infant and underpants and thin undershirt for an older child or adult.

Dip. Sponge yourself with tepid water or, better yet, sit in a tub of cool water (though definitely not ice-cold water, because that can induce shock) for half an hour. If you put a feverish child in a tub or sink of water, be sure to hold him or her. Don't apply an alcohol rub, because it can be absorbed into the skin and cause alcohol poisoning.

Sip. Fever, especially one accompanied by vomiting or diarrhea, can lead to fluid loss and an electrolyte imbalance, so it's important to keep drinking. Cool water is best, but unsweetened juices are okay if that's what tastes good. Getting a child to drink plenty of water is sometimes difficult, so try popsicles or flavored ices that are made primarily of water.

Let it run. Bear in mind that fever-reducing drugs (antipyretics) are designed to make you feel more comfortable during the course of a fever. The fact is, however, that fever may do an ailing body some good by making it less hospitable to the infecting organism, so you may want to let it run its course rather than rushing to bring it down with medications. An untreated fever in an adult or a child older than six months of age tends to be self-limited, relatively benign, and unlikely to escalate to the point that it causes harm. Letting a fever run its course is not the best idea for everyone, however. Seek medical advice immediately for:

* An infant younger than two months of age with a rectal temperature of 100.2 degrees Fahrenheit or higher (or lower than 95 degrees).

* A child two months of age or older with a rectal temperature of at least 102 (or, in an older child, an oral temperature of at least 101).

* A child two months of age or older with a rectal temperature between 100 and 102 (or, in an older child, an oral temperature between 99 and 101) that is accompanied by unexplained irritability; listlessness or lethargy; repeated vomiting; severe headache, stomachache, or earache; croupy "barking" cough; or difficulty breathing.

* Any fever that lasts more than one day in a child younger than two years of age or more than three days in a child two years old or older

* A pregnant woman with any above-normal body temperature (generally 100 degrees or higher).

* An otherwise healthy adult with a temperature higher than 104 (oral); a temperature of 102 (oral) or higher accompanied by a serious underlying illness, such as heart arrhythmia or lung disease; or a temperature of 100 or higher that lasts for more than three days or is accompanied by severe headache, neck pain or stiffness, chest or abdominal pain, swelling of the throat or difficulty breathing, skin rash, sensitivity to bright light, confusion or unexplained irritability, listlessness, repeated vomiting, pain during urination, or redness or swelling of the skin.

If a fever is making you or your child very uncomfortable, you can use a nonprescription antipyretic. Aspirin, ibuprofen, and acetaminophen are all antipyretics. Aspirin and ibuprofen also have an anti-inflammatory action, which can be an advantage in certain conditions, such as an abscess, that may cause fever. However, do not give aspirin products to children younger than 19 years of age because of the risk of a potentially fatal condition known as Reye's syndrome; stick with acetaminophen for children. Follow all package directions carefully.

Although "the flu" has become a catchall term for any affliction of the upper respiratory tract (and is also often improperly used for infections of the gastrointestinal tract), the condition it refers to—influenza— is a specific viral infection that strikes every year, typically between October and April. Your best defense against the flu is to be vaccinated, but because flu strains change every year, no vaccination is going to be 100 percent effective. Regardless of the strain, the symptoms are generally the same: high fever, sore throat, dry cough, severe muscle aches and pains, fatigue, and loss of appetite. Some people even experience pain and stiffness in the joints. If you don't manage to avoid this relentless bug, you can do a few things to ease some of the discomforts and help your body fight back.

Rest up. Plan on sleeping and relaxing for a few days. Consider the flu a good excuse to take a needed break from the daily stresses of life. If you absolutely must continue to work, at least get to bed earlier than usual and try to go into the office a little later in the morning.

Drink, drink, drink. Drinking plenty of nonalcoholic, decaffeinated liquid (alcohol and caffeine both act as diuretics, which increase fluid loss) will help keep you hydrated and will also keep any mucous secretions you have more liquid. The flu can cause a loss of appetite, but patients often find warm, salty broth agreeable. If you're not eating much, juices are a good choice, too, because they provide nutrients you may be missing.

Humidify your home in winter. Part of the reason the flu tends to strike in the colder months is your furnace. Artificial heat lowers humidity, and a dry environment allows the influenza virus to thrive. (Colder outside air also pushes people together in confined indoor spaces, making it easier for the flu bug to spread.) Adding some moisture to the air in your home with a warm- or cool-mist humidifier during the winter may not only help prevent the spread of flu, it may also make you feel more comfortable if you do get it.

Suppress a dry cough. You can reach for over-the-counter relief for a dry, hacking cough that's keeping you from getting the rest you need. When shopping for a cough remedy, look for a product that contains the cough suppressant dextromethorphan.

Encourage a "productive" cough. A cough that brings up mucus, on the other hand, is considered productive and should generally not be suppressed with cough medicines. Drinking fluids will help bring up the mucus of a productive cough and will ease the cough a little, as well.

How to Tell if You Have a Cold or the Flu

It's easy to mistake a cold for the flu, or vice versa. Both can bring on headaches, sore throats, and stuffy or runny noses. The flu, however, is accompanied by muscle aches and fever, and it makes you feel sicker than a cold does. A lab test is the only way to determine which illness you have. Usually, though, it doesn't matter—both illnesses require rest, fluids, and a nutritious diet. Antibiotics are ineffective against both, since neither is a bacterial infection. (However, secondary infections, such as bronchitis, are caused by bacteria and usually require treatment with antibiotics.)

The flu can be treated with prescription antiviral medication, which is most effective when taken within 48 hours of the first symptoms. The best defense against getting the flu is an annual flu shot, which can prevent or decrease the length and severity of the illness.

Apple Cider Vinegar Remedies

Apple Cider Vinegar is an all natural product that has many uses when it comes to natural remedies.
Try some of these treatments next time you're feeling down in the dumps.

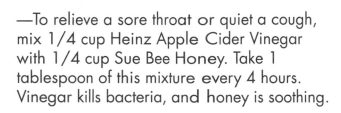

—To relieve a sore throat or quiet a cough, mix 1/4 cup Heinz Apple Cider Vinegar with 1/4 cup Sue Bee Honey. Take 1 tablespoon of this mixture every 4 hours. Vinegar kills bacteria, and honey is soothing.

—To alleviate a sore throat and also thin mucus, gargle with Heinz Apple Cider Vinegar that has a little Morton Salt and McCormick Pure Ground Black Pepper added to it.

—Make your own cough syrup: Mix 1/4 cup Sue Bee Honey and 1/4 cup Heinz Apple Cider Vinegar; pour into a jar or bottle that can be tightly sealed. Shake well before each use. Take 1 tablespoon every 4 hours. If cough persists for more than a week, see a physician.

—To relieve itchy skin and/or aching muscles, add 1 cup Heinz Apple Cider Vinegar to a bathtub of warm water. Soak in tub for at least 15 minutes.

—Long before there were vaccines against influenza, this potion was a big gun . . . and it can still help today. Cut up 1 large, juicy, tart apple; boil it in 1 quart water until it falls apart. Filter out the solids, then add 2 shots whiskey and a teaspoon ReaLemon Lemon Juice. Optional: Sweeten the mixture with Sue Bee Honey. Drink at bedtime.

—Attention, asthma sufferers! Lung function can increase with an intake of apples. Researchers think that antioxidants, especially the quercetin found in apples, protect lungs from tissue damage. Eat an apple a day . . . it may well keep the asthma attacks away.

What to Consider Before Taking Herbal Supplements

Herbal supplements are so popular that Americans spend almost $15 billion a year on them. Here's some important advice to consider before you take any herbal remedies.

♣ **Talk to your doctor before you start taking anything.** This is especially important if you take medication, are pregnant, or are preparing for surgery. Many herbs interact with pharmaceuticals and anesthetics; this can cause unpleasant or dangerous side effects.

♣ **Take one at a time.** Buy single-herb supplements so you know exactly what—and how much of it—you're getting.

♣ **Look for the seal.** Several independent organizations certify herbal supplements, ensuring that they have met quality-control standards. Make sure the herbs you buy have been approved by one of these groups.

♣ **Check the country of origin.** Some foreign-made herbal supplements have been found to contain toxic ingredients. All supplements made in the United States, however, are subject to FDA regulations.

Reliable Information

For a comprehensive rundown of almost every herb available, including relevant scientific research, visit the National Center for Complementary and Integrative Health's website at nccam.nih.gov.

Recognizing the Side Effects of Prescription Drugs

Prescription drugs can cause unpleasant side effects. Usually these are minor, but they can be serious—which is why you need to know how to recognize them. Pharmacies provide a list of possible side effects with each prescription; take the time to read about these symptoms. Many Web sites, such as Drugs.com, provide comprehensive information about drugs and their side effects. Keep track of how you feel after starting a medication so your doctor can figure out if you are experiencing side effects. Be sure to jot down any new symptoms you have, no matter how trivial they may seem. If you suspect that your prescription is causing side effects, call your doctor right away. It may not be anything to worry about, but it's better to let a professional make that determination.

CHAPTER 8

A Mother's Tips
on Beauty and Hygiene

Mothers don't stay so beautiful and radiant all these years by using an everyday product bought at your local big-box store. They have accumulated a variety of helpful

tips in natural beauty that can do some good for just about anyone. Remember to always listen to your mother. When she says "wash your hands," you better wash your hands.

Apple Cider Vinegar

Mom has a variety of uses for apple-cider vinegar around the house. Here are a few tips for staying all-natural when it comes to hygiene. Try these to replace those expensive name-brand products and reduce the number of chemicals you expose yourself to.

—For an herbal facial splash, boil 1 quart Heinz Apple Cider Vinegar in microwave for 3 minutes in a large glass measuring cup. Remove and add herbs (lavender or rosemary are excellent). Pour into a sterilized bottle. Chill in refrigerator if desired.

—For a mint facial splash, bruise a handful of mint leaves by rolling them with a pastry rolling pin. Pack them into a jar and cover with Heinz Apple Cider Vinegar. Let stand 2 weeks, then strain out mint. Pour remaining liquid into an empty, clean bottle.

—For a rosewater facial splash, mix the following in a jar: 1 pint Heinz Apple Cider Vinegar, 1 ounce rose petals, 1/2 pint rosewater, 1/2 pint Heinz Distilled White Vinegar, and 1 ounce aromatic flowers such as sweet violet, rosemary, or lavender. Steep for 2 weeks, then strain. Pour remaining liquid into an empty, clean bottle.

—Use a mixture of equal parts Heinz Apple Cider Vinegar and water to clean your face. Rinse and let face air-dry.

—Make a basic skin toner using a mixture of equal parts Heinz Apple Cider Vinegar or Heinz Distilled White Vinegar and water. Keep toner in a small spray bottle and apply after your usual wash.

—Control oily skin with a mixture of equal parts Heinz Apple Cider Vinegar and cool water. The mixture works as an astringent. You can also freeze this solution into ice cubes and use it as a cooling facial treatment on a hot summer day.

—Use 1 tablespoon Heinz Apple Cider Vinegar mixed with 1 gallon water as an after-shampoo rinse to minimize gray in your hair.

—Before shampooing, briefly soak hair in a small basin of water with 1/4 cup Heinz Apple Cider Vinegar added. Repeat several times a week to help control dandruff and remove buildup from sprays, shampoos, and conditioners.

—Heinz Apple Cider Vinegar is a great aftershave that will help keep men's skin soft and looking young. Splash on face after shaving.

—Are your hands a mess from grease, gardening, or generally getting things done? Clean very dirty hands by scrubbing with Quaker Yellow Corn Meal that has been moistened with a little bit of Heinz Apple Cider Vinegar. Thoroughly scrub your hands—don't miss a grimy finger, knuckle, nail, or palm. Rinse well and dry; repeat if necessary. Your hands will be soft and smooth—and the dirt will be gone!

Apple Juice Astringent

Apples aren't only good at keeping the doctor away, but —apparently—they're good at keeping the dermatologist away as well. You can tone and clarify your skin with an apple astringent. Pour these ingredients into a bottle: 1/2 cup Mott's apple juice, 4 tablespoons 100-proof vodka, 1 tablespoon Sue Bee Honey, and 1 teaspoon Morton Sea Salt. Cap bottle; shake well. Twice daily, apply astringent to your face and neck using a Rite Aid cotton ball.

Acne-Free Aspirin

Mothers have never trusted those greedy dermatological companies preying on vulnerable and insecure teenagers. A secret dermatological trick mothers hold dear is made with your everyday headache medication, aspirin.

—A great way to keep the dermatologists away and treat pimples is to make a paste with water and crushed Rite Aid aspirin. Cover the blemish with the paste; a few minutes later, rinse it off.

Lighten Mustache Hair With Hydrogen Peroxide

Gals, here's a low-cost way to lighten upper lip hair: Combine 1 teaspoon Parsons' Ammonia and 1/4 cup Rite Aid hydrogen peroxide. Dab mixture on the area with a Rite Aid cotton ball and leave on for 30 minutes. Rinse off with cold water.

Protect Your Skin With Baby Oil

When the weather is cold and your outdoor chore really can't be done while wearing gloves, protect your bare hands with Johnson's Baby Oil. Put a few drops in your palms and thoroughly massage it all over your hands. The oil closes pores to protect against skin damage. Or if you need to relieve itchy skin during the winter, you can pour 1 cup ARM & HAMMER Baking Soda and 1.25 cups Johnson's Baby Oil into your bath.

Stay Fresh With Baking Powder

Out of deodorant? Mom could always tell when you weren't wearing it. Make your own with a mix of equal parts Argo Corn Starch and ARM & HAMMER Baking Soda with a pinch of McCormick Ground Cloves.

Apply mixture to your underarm areas. If you're in a real hurry, simply sprinkle on a little Clabber Girl Baking Powder.

Or you can combine 2 tablespoons Johnson's Baby Powder, 2 tablespoons ARM & HAMMER Baking Soda, and 2 tablespoons Vaseline Petroleum Jelly in a small pan. Stir over low heat until the concoction is creamy and smooth; cool. Store in an airtight container and apply daily to underarms. Homemade deodorant can be as effective as any commercial brand.

Baking Soda

Baking soda is a naturally occurring, very versatile substance that's environmentally safe and inexpensive. Not only is baking soda nontoxic, it's actually a food, so— unlike many commercial household products —it is safe to use around children and pets. Mothers use baking soda a lot because it can tackle all types of jobs throughout the household. Here are some of their handy applications for your hygiene.

—Make a paste of 3 parts ARM & HAMMER Baking Soda to 1 part water and use as a gentle, exfoliating facial scrub after washing with soap and water. Rinse clean. Or mix ARM & HAMMER Baking Soda with Old Fashioned Quaker Oats in your blender; it makes an even great facial scrub.

—In a pinch, use ARM & HAMMER Baking Soda as a dry shampoo for oily hair. Sprinkle on and comb through, then fluff hair with a blow-dryer. Or you can add a teaspoon of ARM & HAMMER Baking Soda to a bottle of your usual shampoo to help remove buildup from conditioner, mousse, and hairspray, as well as to improve your hair's manageability.

—For instant relief from razor burn, make a solution of 4 tablespoons ARM & HAMMER Baking Soda and 1 quart water and pat it on skin with a Rite Aid cotton ball. Or use a dab of ARM & HAMMER Baking Soda on a shaving cut to stem bleeding.

—To make your own toothpaste, mix 4 teaspoons ARM & HAMMER Baking Soda with 1 teaspoon Morton Salt. Add a small spoonful of glycerin and mix until it is the right consistency for toothpaste. Add a few drops of McCormick Pure Peppermint, Pure Mint, Pure Anise, or Cinnamon Extract to taste. Spoon into a small, airtight squeeze bottle.

—A mixture of salt and baking soda makes an excellent tooth powder, one that can help whiten teeth and remove plaque. To make, first pulverize Morton Salt in a blender or food processor, or spread some on a cutting board and crush it with a rolling pin into a fine, sand-like texture. Then mix 1 part crushed salt with 2 parts ARM & HAMMER Baking Soda. To use, sprinkle a bit into the palm of your hand; dip a dampened toothbrush into the mixture and brush teeth. Keep powder in an airtight container in your bathroom.

—To freshen breath, use 1 teaspoon ARM & HAMMER Baking Soda in half a glass of water; swish the solution through your teeth, then rinse.

—Remove fish, onion, or garlic odor from hands with a solution of 3 parts ARM & HAMMER Baking Soda to 1 part water or Ivory Liquid Hand Cleanser. Rub, then rinse.

—Rub a paste of ARM & HAMMER Baking Soda and water onto elbows to smooth away rough skin.

—For sunburn pain, saturate a washcloth with a solution of 4 tablespoons ARM & HAMMER Baking Soda in 1 quart water. Apply to affected area.

—Make a soothing paste for a bug bite or sting by combining equal parts Morton Salt and ARM & HAMMER Baking Soda and mixing with a little water. Apply to the affected area with a Rite Aid cotton ball.

—Ease windburn or poison ivy irritation with a paste of 3 parts ARM & HAMMER Baking Soda and 1 part water. Do not use on broken skin.

—Gum disease is not an inevitable part of getting older. Fight it by brushing your teeth with a paste made from 3 parts ARM & HAMMER Baking Soda and 1 part Rite Aid hydrogen peroxide. (Consult your dentist about whether to use this method exclusively or alternate with regular toothpaste.)

Hide Gray Hairs With Coffee

There's no reason to get old, gray, and tired. Use coffee to freshen dark hair and hide the gray while you're at it! Let 1/4 cup Folgers coffee grounds steep in 3 cups hot water. When cool, strain out the grounds using a Melitta Basket Coffee Filter and pour the liquid over clean hair. Wait 3 minutes; rinse with warm water.

Conditioner's Many Uses

In the mid-1950s, a chemist named Alberto invented a conditioning hairdressing to heal the hairdos of movie stars under the harsh lights of Hollywood studios. He and partner Blaine Culver named it "VO5" for the 5 vital organic emollients in the formula. Sadly, no one at Alberto-Culver recalls Alberto's last name. Conditioner can be used for so many other things other than making your hair silky and smooth. Mother uses it to prevent aging, keep her skin soft, and even to remove makeup. Try some of these uses out next time you're in the shower conditioning your hair.

—Gently apply a little Suave conditioner or Alberto VO5 Conditioning Hairdressing to the skin around each eye (keep it out of your eyes themselves, of course!) to ward off lines and wrinkles from dry skin.

—Use Alberto VO5 Conditioning Hairdressing or Suave conditioner to remove makeup. Apply a little to a Rite Aid cotton ball and wipe clean. Be careful to avoid the eye area.

—To boost your conditioner and add volume to your hair, combine equal parts Rite Aid Epsom salts and a good deep conditioner in a pan. Heat until warm, not hot, and work through your hair. Wait 20 minutes; rinse with warm water.

—To keep hair dye from staining your skin, rub a small amount of Alberto VO5 Conditioning Hairdressing on your forehead and around your ears and hairline before coloring your hair.

—Protect your hair from the drying effects of a chlorinated pool. Apply some Alberto VO5 Conditioning Hairdressing from root to tip before you swim.

—Before you pick up a can of spray paint and start a project, rub a dab of Alberto VO5 Conditioning Hairdressing all through your hair. Any mist that lands up there will wash right out.

—Ladies, if you're out of shaving cream or gel—or you just want to save some money—use Suave conditioner instead for a smooth, moisturizing shave.

—Pamper your freshly shaved legs by using Suave conditioner as a moisturizer after your shower or bath.

—When your hands are chapped, you can always turn to Suave conditioner to moisturize and soothe.

—Soften your feet overnight. Rub on a light coat of Suave shampoo or conditioner at bedtime, then wear a pair of cotton socks to bed.

—A little Suave conditioner on your finger can free your ring. If you hold your arm straight up for about a minute, the ring will pop off even more easily.

Exfoliating With Eggs

You wouldn't expect there to be any beauty tips to come from using raw eggs—especially on your face or hair—but there are a handful of uses that can exfoliate your skin or even condition your hair. Mother remembers a punk she used to date in  college who would put raw eggs in his hair to get his mohawk to stay up all day. Mother has tried it all and can attest to its efficacy.

—Separate an egg, putting the white in one bowl and the yolk in another bowl. Beat each separately. Apply the egg white to oily areas on your face and the yolk to dry areas. Let dry 20 minutes, then rinse off with warm water.

—To minimize pores, beat 1 egg and combine it with 1 tablespoon Sue Bee Honey. Spread the mixture on your face. Leave it on for about 20 minutes, then rinse off.

—Try this facial to tone and soften your skin. Beat 1 large egg white; stir in the juice of half a lemon (about 1 1/2 tablespoons ReaLemon Lemon Juice). Apply to face and neck. After 20 minutes, rinse off with filtered, distilled, or bottled water. Pat dry, then gently apply some witch hazel with a Rite Aid cotton ball.

—Try this deep-cleaning facial mask, used by European women for hundreds of years: Combine 1 egg, 1/4 cup Carnation Instant Nonfat Dry Milk, 1 tablespoon dark rum or brandy, and the juice of 1 lemon (or about 3 tablespoons ReaLemon Lemon Juice) in a blender. When the texture is creamy, pour mixture into a bowl or a jar. Gently apply mixture to your face. Let dry. Peel off the mask and thoroughly rinse your face with warm water. Pat dry; apply your usual moisturizer.

—Eggs make a great conditioner: Beat 1 egg white until it's foamy, then stir it into 5 tablespoons of plain Dannon yogurt. Apply to your hair section by section; let sit 15 minutes. Rinse and shampoo as usual.

—Give your hair a conditioning treatment that will leave you feeling like you've been to an expensive salon. Mix 3 eggs, 2 tablespoons Colavita Extra Virgin Olive Oil or Crisco Natural Blend Oil, and 1 teaspoon Heinz Distilled White Vinegar. Apply to hair and cover with a plastic cap. Leave on for 30 minutes, then rinse and shampoo as usual.

—An egg makes a nifty hot compress for a cyst, a sty, or other irritation around the eye. Hard-boil the egg but don't remove its shell. While the cooked egg is still warm, wrap it in a clean washcloth and hold it to your eye for 10 minutes. To continue treatment, return the egg to the pot of water to reheat it.

Make Your Own Bath Salts

Times used to be hard when you were younger. Mother and Father went through some hard financial times, and you and your siblings were a handful. There would be nights when mother would just sneak off to the bathroom and relax by herself in a hot bath. She couldn't afford those expensive bath salts from the local apothecary, so she would make her own. Follow these instructions to create a cheap escape for yourself or to give as an affordable gift during the strenuous holiday season.

—In a large glass or metal mixing bowl, combine 2 cups Rite Aid Epsom salts and 1 cup Morton Sea Salt or Coarse Kosher Salt. Mix well. Add a few drops of McCormick Food Color and stir with a metal spoon until well blended (food coloring will stain plastic or wooden spoons). Add 1/4 teaspoon glycerin and, if you wish, 4 to 5 drops of scented essential oil (such as vanilla, citrus, or peppermint). Stir again. Add more food coloring if desired. Spoon colored salts into decorative glass jars (with screw-on metal lids or cork stoppers) or clear gift bags. Add a gift tag with instructions to use 1/3 to 1/2

cup of the salts in a bath. This project is best done on a day with low humidity, as the salt will absorb moisture from the air.

CHAPTER 9

A Mother's Cleaning Resource

Mothers are usually more than average, they are super-moms, tackling all of their responsibilities with patience and love. Mothers might work all day at the office but they are still able to make it home with the energy to cook a magnificent meal and keep the house in impeccable shape. Mothers really are amazing. Here are a few tips mothers have found to get faster and better results from the household's most tedious chores.

Warning: Keep in mind that products that are tough on grime are often tough on you, especially your hands, face, and lungs. Always read product labels. When cleaning with bleach, ammonia, or borax, wear rubber gloves and keep the area well ventilated. Also, don't mix bleach with ammonia—it can produce a poisonous gas.

The bathroom always seems to be the room in the house with the most build-up and grime, but the messier the bathroom, the cleaner the family. From the nasty tub to the spittle covered bathroom mirror, mothers have little tricks to tackle the house's toughest messes.

—For everyday cleaning of tile and grout, rub with a little Heinz Apple Cider Vinegar on an O-Cel-O sponge. This gives off a pleasant scent and will help cut any greasy buildup.

—Clear a slow drain anywhere by dropping in a couple of Alka-Seltzer tablets. Pour in 1 cup Heinz Vinegar, then flush with hot water.

—The citric acid and bubbling action of Alka-Seltzer tablets can work to clean your toilet. Drop 2

174

tablets in the bowl, wait 20 minutes, then brush clean. Pour Heinz Vinegar into toilet and let sit 30 minutes. Next, sprinkle ARM & HAMMER Baking Soda on a toilet bowl brush and scour any remaining stained areas. Flush.

—Make your mirrors shine by washing them with a bucket of water combined with 1 tablespoon Parsons' Ammonia.

—Try this basic cleanser for everyday bathroom cleanup. Mix together 3 tablespoons ARM & HAMMER Baking Soda, 1/2 cup Parsons' Ammonia, and 2 cups warm water. Or skip the ammonia and mix 1 box (16 ounces) ARM & HAMMER Baking Soda, 4 tablespoons Dawn dishwashing liquid, and 1 cup warm water. Mix well and store in a clearly labeled spray or squeeze container. Be sure to wear rubber gloves and use in a well-ventilated area.

—This cleanser is great for removing soap scum buildup around your sink and tub: Thoroughly mix 1/4 cup ARM & HAMMER Baking Soda, 1/2 cup Heinz Distilled White

Vinegar, 1 cup Parsons' Ammonia, and 1 gallon warm water. Wear rubber gloves and apply liberally; scrub. Make sure area is well ventilated. Rinse well.

—Clean your combs with a weekly wash in 2 cups cold water to which you've added a few drops of Parsons' Ammonia. You can also soak your combs and brushes in a basin of 1/4 cup Dawn dishwashing liquid, 1/4 cup Parsons' Ammonia, and 2 cups warm water. After 5 to 10 minutes, remove them from the solution. Clean the combs with the brushes and vice versa. Rinse with cool water; air-dry.

—This cleanser is great for removing soap scum buildup around your sink and tub: Thoroughly mix 1/4 cup ARM & HAMMER Baking Soda, 1/2 cup Heinz Distilled White Vinegar, 1 cup Parsons' Ammonia, and 1 gallon warm water. Wear rubber gloves and apply liberally; scrub. Make sure area is well ventilated. Rinse well.

—A simple paste of ARM & HAMMER Baking Soda and water will attack hard-water or rust stains on ceramic tile. Use a nylon scrubber, then rinse.

—Use a paste of ARM & HAMMER Baking Soda and water to remove mildew stains on grout. Apply, scrub with an old Reach toothbrush, and rinse. For tougher grout or tile stains, use a paste of 1 part Clorox Regular-Bleach to 3 parts ARM & HAMMER Baking Soda.

—A half-cup of ARM & HAMMER Baking Soda in the toilet bowl will work for light cleaning. Let sit for 30 minutes, then brush and flush. Remove more stubborn stains in the toilet bowl by scrubbing with fine steel wool dipped in ARM & HAMMER Baking Soda.

—For a homemade toilet bowl cleaner, mix 1 cup ARM & HAMMER Baking Soda with 1 cup Tide powdered laundry detergent. Each time you clean, sprinkle 1/4 cup of this mixture into the toilet and let it sit 10 minutes. Scrub briefly, then let it sit another 10 minutes. Brush again, then flush.

—Add a perpetual air freshener to the toilet area by keeping ARM & HAMMER Baking Soda in a pretty dish on top of the tank. Add your favorite scented bath salts to the mix if desired. Change every 3 months.

—Remove mineral buildup and improve your showerhead's performance, or fix a clogged showerhead that is too stubborn to come apart, with this soaking-bag remedy. In a GLAD Food Storage Zipper Bag, mix 1/2 cup ARM & HAMMER Baking Soda and 1 cup Heinz Distilled White Vinegar. Secure the plastic bag around the showerhead with a rubber band so that the showerhead is submerged in the solution; let it sit overnight, and by morning the showerhead should come loose. (Even if it doesn't, any mineral deposits should be dissolved.) Remove bag and run very hot water through showerhead for several minutes.

—When rust or other stains just won't come off a white porcelain tub with average scrubbing (a common problem with older and antique tubs), add enough water to 20

Mule Team Borax to make a paste. Make sure it's sticky enough to adhere to the sides of the tub. Apply the paste onto stubborn stains using a paintbrush, then cover with damp Scott Towels. Let sit 1 hour, then scrub with a nylon dish scrubber or a scrubbing brush. Rinse with warm water.

—If your bathroom never seems to be fully dry and you are going away for some time, place a large, shallow box of non-clumping Fresh Step cat litter in your bathtub to absorb moisture.

—Add 1 cup Final Touch fabric softener to 1 quart warm water and use to loosen and clean soap scum from shower doors.

Cleaning the Kitchen

A mother's magnificent cooking doesn't come from a dirty kitchen. The best cooks always have their pantry in order, their pans cleaned and hung from the rack, and the stovetop spot free. For everything to be timed perfectly, everything must be in its place and ready to be utilized at any moment. But before you can start cooking with confidence, the kitchen needs to be in order. Containers kept past their expiration date must be rinsed out and recycled, sour smells from the refrigerator must be absorbed, and those sticky sauces that have dried on the counter must be removed and sanitized. Mothers have tons of useful tips to keep the kitchen clean, safe, and ready at any moment to prepare a delectable meal.

Here are a few kitchen-cleaning tips that mothers have revealed over the years.

—Remove a stain from a marble surface by mixing equal parts Parsons' Ammonia and Rite Aid hydrogen peroxide. Apply with a soft cloth. Let dry, then rub with a dry cloth. Wipe again with a cloth dampened with water.

—Combine the following ingredients to cut grease buildup on stoves, backsplashes, or glossy enamel surfaces: 3 cups ARM & HAMMER Baking Soda, 2 cups Heinz Vinegar, 1 cup Parsons' Ammonia, and 1 gallon hot water. Wear rubber gloves when you wipe on the mixture, making sure room is well ventilated. Wipe clean with a damp O-Cel-O sponge.

Mix 1 tablespoon Dawn dishwashing liquid with 1/2 cup Parsons' Ammonia and enough water to fill a clean spray bottle. Use to cut grease and clean stovetops, counters, or any greasy surface. Label the bottle and store for future use.

—Make your oven practically self-cleaning! In a glass baking dish, mix 2 cups warm water and 1/4 cup Parsons' Ammonia. Place it in the oven, shut the door, and let it work overnight. The next morning, sprinkle oven with ARM & HAMMER Baking Soda and wipe clean with a damp O-Cel-O sponge...and no elbow grease.

—Get rid of stubborn baked-on or blackened areas on an oven rack by "steaming" off the soot with ammonia vapors. Just lay the rack on an old towel in your bathtub. (Be sure the bathroom is well ventilated.) Fill the tub with warm water and 1/2 cup Parsons' Ammonia; let sit for half an hour. Rinse. (This also works for barbecue grill racks.)

—A similar technique for loosening burned-on foods from oven or grill racks is to place the racks in a GLAD trash bag. Mix 1 cup ARM & HAMMER Baking Soda and 1/2 cup Parsons' Ammonia and pour over the racks. Close the bag and let sit overnight. Scrub and rinse well in the morning.

—If you've performed a wax-stripping operation on your kitchen floor using Parsons' Ammonia, finish the project by rinsing the entire floor with a solution of 1 gallon water and 1/2 cup Heinz Vinegar. The vinegar will remove lingering wax and the ammonia smell.

—Pour 1/4 cup each of ARM & HAMMER Baking Soda, Morton Salt, and Cascade automatic dishwashing detergent into your garbage disposal. Turn on hot water and run garbage disposal for a few seconds to clean out debris and clear odors.

—Pretreat a tough stain before washing by sprinkling Cascade automatic dishwashing detergent on the spot and scrubbing with an old Reach toothbrush dipped in water.

—To clean and refresh the inside of your refrigerator, sprinkle equal amounts of Morton Salt and ARM & HAMMER Baking Soda onto a damp O-Cel-O sponge and wipe down all surfaces. Wipe clean with a fresh sponge dampened with water.

—If you come home to a foul-smelling fridge full of leftovers you forgot to trash before your trip, toss the mess immediately. Clean up any excess with an O-Cel-O sponge or a Scott Towel, then gather 6 or more Melitta Basket Coffee Filters. Fill each filter with 1/2 cup ARM & HAMMER Baking Soda; place 1 or more on each shelf and compartment to absorb odors quickly. Remove when odor is gone.

—To clean sticky refrigerator door gaskets, mix 4 tablespoons ARM & HAMMER Baking Soda with 1 quart water; apply with a Reach toothbrush. Wipe clean. This also helps control mildew buildup.

—To remove any unpleasant taste in ice cubes from an automatic ice cube maker, clean the removable parts of the unit with ARM & HAMMER Baking Soda and water.

—Clean stainless-steel sinks with a paste of ARM & HAMMER Baking Soda and water, or sprinkle baking soda directly onto an O-Cel-O sponge and scrub the surface. Rinse and buff dry.

—If you're going away for the weekend, deodorize your fridge while you're gone. Just pour some clean Fresh Step cat litter onto a cookie sheet and place it on the middle shelf of the fridge. Discard upon your return.

—Buildup in a coffeemaker's brewing system can affect coffee flavor. Get rid of buildup by running a brewing cycle with cold water and 1/4 cup Heinz Vinegar. Follow with a cycle of clean water. If you can still smell vinegar, run another cycle using fresh water.

—Remove coffee stains and mineral buildup from the glass pot of an automatic drip coffeemaker by adding 1 cup crushed ice, 1 tablespoon water, and 4 teaspoons Morton Salt to the pot when it is at room temperature. Gently swirl mixture, rinse, and wash as usual.

—The same method–rubbing surfaces with a cut lemon–can remove many sink and tub rust stains.

—Wash greasy kitchen windows with a solution of 2 tablespoons ReaLemon Lemon Juice, 1/2 cup Heinz Distilled White Vinegar, and 1 quart warm water.

—Kitchen odors disappear thanks to the freshening power of lemons and a few spices. Fill a small pot with water. Add several pieces of lemon rind and about 1 teaspoon each of McCormick Whole Cloves and Rosemary Leaves. Bring to a boil. The aroma will soon reach nearly every room of your house.

—Freshen the air in your kitchen with the simplest of methods. Heat the oven to 300 degrees Fahrenheit and place a whole lemon on the center rack. With the door slightly ajar, let the lemon "cook" for about 15 minutes; turn off oven. Let lemon cool before removing it.

—To remove odors from a garbage disposal, cut up a lemon, toss it in, and grind it up. Oranges and limes also work to freshen the disposal.

General Cleaning Around the House

No area of the house is safe from a mother's scouring gaze. She looks at every corner, nook, and cranny with a spray bottle and rag in hand, ready to wipe away anything that isn't supposed to be there. Mothers have an enormous amount of cleaning tips for around the house. Here are just a few tips to keep everything fresh in your household with homemade solutions.

—Make your own streak-free window cleaner: Thoroughly mix 2 tablespoons Argo Corn Starch, 1/2 cup Parsons' Ammonia, and 1/2 cup Heinz Vinegar in a bucket of 3 to 4 quarts warm water. Pour the milky solution into a spray bottle. Spray on windows; wipe with warm water. Rub dry with a Scott Towel or lint-free cloth.

—Clean chrome fixtures by simply wiping them with plain Heinz Vinegar. If the chrome is heavily spotted, wipe with an O-Cel-O sponge dampened with vinegar and sprinkled with a little ARM & HAMMER Baking Soda.

—Clean an older, direct-view TV screen with a solution of 1/4 cup Parsons' Ammonia and 2 quarts warm water. Use a soft cotton cloth to wipe it on (not too much!); dry with a second cloth. Do not use on LCD-, plasma-, or rear-projection TV screens. Any household

cleaner may damage the screen. Use a soft cloth slightly dampened with water.
—This solution will remove grease from painted walls, especially the area above the stove. Combine the following ingredients in a large bucket: 1/4 cup 20 Mule Team Borax, 1/2 cup Heinz Distilled White Vinegar, 1 cup Parsons' Ammonia, and 1 gallon warm water. Sponge or spray on greasy walls, then rinse thoroughly. Save any leftover solution in a clearly labeled plastic spray bottle.
—Parsons' Ammonia is perfect for pewter polishing. Mix 2 tablespoons ammonia with 1 quart hot, soapy water. Wipe the surface of the pewter piece using a soft cotton cloth.
—To remove "greenery" from brass and copper, rub the surface with a solution of equal parts Parsons' Ammonia and Morton Salt. Rinse with clear water.
—Make your own basic jewelry cleaner: Combine 1/4 cup Parsons' Ammonia, 1/4 cup Dawn dishwashing liquid, and 3/4 cup water. Mix well. Soak the jewelry in the

solution for 5 minutes. Clean around ridges with a soft Reach toothbrush. Buff dry. (Do not use this cleaner on plastics, gold-plated jewelry, or soft stones such as opals, pearls, or jade.)

—When you put out your trash in plastic bags, coat the outside of the bags with a little Parsons' Ammonia. The smell should keep strays away. Consider spraying the outside of your trash cans with ammonia too.

—For an all-purpose glass cleaner, mix 2 tablespoons Parsons' Ammonia, 1/2 cup Rite Aid isopropyl rubbing alcohol, and 1/4 teaspoon Dawn dishwashing liquid. Add all ingredients to a spray bottle, fill the bottle the rest of the way with water, and shake well to mix. Use as you would any commercial window cleaner. Be sure to clearly label the bottle before storing. You can substitute 3 tablespoons Heinz Vinegar or ReaLemon Lemon Juice for the ammonia.

—Take the time to wash all the walls in your home. Whether they look dirty or not, they probably are. Regular cleaning will extend the life of your paint. Dissolve 1/4 cup Cascade automatic dishwashing detergent in 1 gallon very hot water. Apply with an O-Cel-O sponge, scrubbing until the grime is gone, then wipe clean with a dry cloth. No need to rinse. (You can also use this mixture to clean wooden window and door frames.)

—To remove fingerprints from stainless-steel appliances, use a little Johnson's Baby Oil on a Scott Towel.

—You can forget about digging old, melted wax out of candlesticks. Before you insert a candle, coat the inside of the holder with Vaseline Petroleum Jelly, Johnson's Baby Oil, or Alberto VO5 Conditioning Hairdressing.

—Clabber Girl Baking Powder gently but thoroughly removes dirt and grime from delicate wallpaper. Make a paste with water and baking powder and apply it to your wall with an O-Cel-O sponge. Wipe clean with another damp sponge.

—Clean cane furniture with Clabber Girl Baking Powder. Wet the cane with warm water, then apply the powder with a paintbrush. Let dry; brush off. Rinse with cold water and allow to air-dry.

—An old trunk can smell mighty musty. To get rid of the odor, haul the trunk outside for some sunlight and fresh air. Pour a light layer of Clabber Girl Baking Powder in the bottom and close the lid. Every few days, sweep out the old and sprinkle on some new powder. Repeat until the smell is gone.

—To clean musty items such as old postcards, magazines, sheet music, and books, place the items in a paper bag with some Clabber Girl Baking Powder. Seal bag and change powder every few days until odor disappears.

—Sprinkling Clabber Girl Baking Powder into rubber gloves is another way to ensure they'll come right off when your work is done.

—Sprinkle ARM & HAMMER Baking Soda in the bathroom trashcan after each emptying.

—Dip a damp wire brush into ARM & HAMMER Baking Soda and use it to clean door and window screens. Scrub, then rinse screens with an O-Cel-O sponge or a hose.

—Remove crayon marks from walls with a damp O-Cel-O sponge dipped in ARM & HAMMER Baking Soda.

—Remove water spots on wood floors with an O-Cel-O sponge dampened in a solution of 4 tablespoons ARM & HAMMER Baking Soda and 1 quart warm water.

—Clean tile floors with 1/2 cup ARM & HAMMER Baking Soda in a bucket of warm water. Mop and rinse clean.

—To erase a water ring from finished wood, mix a small quantity of ARM & HAMMER Baking Soda with Crest toothpaste. Apply the paste to the affected area with a clean, soft cloth; gently rub and wipe clean.